What people are saying ab

HOW TO QUIET A HURRICANE

"A powerful reminder, encouragement and challenge on finishing the race, completing the task, and going the distance. Justin provides a timely road map for living and leading above and beyond the mundane, bland, and boring. Steer into a new lane of life marked by God's power, breakthrough, miracle-working faith, and expectation."

Brad Lomenick, founder of BLINC and author
of *H3 Leadership* and *The Catalyst Leader*

"Though more options and autonomy have not delivered on the happiness we had hoped to receive, rather than relying on the usual prescription of '10 Steps to Finding Happiness,' Justin Kendrick invites us to go deeper with God. God offers a different way to do life. Drawing us in with stories, both biblical and personal, Justin guides us down a path that brings endurance and joy in a world that keeps throwing us curveballs."

David Ashcraft, president and CEO
of Global Leadership Network and
author of *What Was I Thinking?*

"A mentor once told me that we are remembered more by our exits from life than our entries in life, but with the assistance of Justin's book, I've come to believe that we are remembered more by our endurance through life. In *How to Quiet a Hurricane*, we are not given the typical 'add water and stir' approach to contending with the inescapable challenges of life, nor are we served an unrealistic and robotic call to persevere brainlessly through our suffering. Instead, this book provides readers with biblical and practical steps to help readers remain buoyant in even the worst of storms. Sometimes life's obstacles can make us feel insane and in need of an old-fashioned straitjacket. One read through this book and you'll see that you've been given a life jacket."

Wayne Francis, lead pastor of The Life Church NY, coauthor of *God and Race*, and chaplain of the Brooklyn Nets

"The hurricanes of life come in a variety of shapes, sizes, and intensity. And they are inescapable. Justin Kendrick masterfully and biblically helps us shift our perspective about the hurricanes of hardship. What if pain and suffering weren't the enemy, but rather the pathway to a life of supernatural power? This thoughtful and practical book will equip you to walk through the hurricanes and come out the other side with your love for Jesus stronger than ever."

Lance Witt, founder of Replenish Ministries

"*How to Quiet a Hurricane* is a practical and eye-opening book that compels readers to take an introspective look at themselves while evaluating their lives, particularly amid challenges and the relentless pressures of modern society. Through thoughtful examples and biblical accounts, this book makes a solid case that having sincere faith in God is the only way that we are able to grow, endure, and ultimately live a victorious and abundant life. In a world where so many are giving up, *How to Quiet a Hurricane* is a much-needed reminder that through life's storms, we possess the power to find stillness within and a life of joy when we look for opportunities to operate in the word of God and walk in his strength."

John K. Jenkins, senior pastor of First
Baptist Church of Glenarden, Maryland

"How to Quiet a Hurricane is a must-read for finding peace in the storm and deepening your relationship with Christ. If you're maneuvering through a minefield of stress or challenges, Justin Kendrick delivers practical and biblical applications of what to do when the caffeine and adrenaline have worn off and you've reached your limit. This book is for those who are tired of struggling in their own power to stay afloat and want to delve deep into the wellspring of life for peace and certainty. Kendrick offers revolutionary insights into the faith, providing biblical methods and spiritual weapons to endure trials, abide in God's love, and stand with the clarity of who we are in Jesus. *How to Quiet a Hurricane* will change your thinking about how to navigate rough waters and who's at the helm."

Deryck C. Frye, president of Connect
United Inc. and lead pastor of Connect
Church, Ashland, Massachusetts

"Rich, brilliant, heartfelt, honest, and sincere are just a few of the words that kept coming to my mind as I read this amazing book by Justin Kendrick! Justin takes us on a journey not only through his personal life experiences but also through *God's Word* in an intriguing and compelling way. I was drawn in to this journey and found enrichment in my own spiritual life through these words and my time in the Bible. I truly believe that this book is appointed for such a time as this!"

Rev. Anthony Milas, lead pastor
of Granite United Church

"Our culture is awash in fear right now. People of faith are being shaken by gale-force winds of anxiety, depression, and digital overwhelm. Into this howling hurricane, Jesus speaks. Not loudly, just a whisper: *Abide in me.* In *How to Quiet a Hurricane*, Justin Kendrick charts the course to God's promise of peace and supernatural power in the midst of crisis. Turns out peace doesn't come from the absence of conflict—but the presence of Christ within it! Ready to speak to your storm? Read this powerful book!"

Tim Lucas, lead pastor and
author of *Liquid Church*

"In *How to Quiet a Hurricane*, Justin Kendrick breaks open his own soul and allows the reader to feed upon the love of Christ that has sustained and nurtured him in his own journey of faith. Rich in biblical teaching and clear theological truth, and amplified by the insights of a broad sampling of other seasoned travelers, this book is a reliable guide for anyone seeking to navigate the quest of faith in today's world. It is solid truth, it is accessible, and it is helpful! And I can say that I have seen it lived out in the life of the author. I recommend this book heartily!"

Rev. Rick McKinniss, senior pastor of
Wellspring Church, Berlin, Connecticut

HOW TO QUIET A HURRICANE

HOW TO QUIET A HURRICANE

STRATEGIES FOR CHRISTIAN ENDURANCE IN THE MIDST OF LIFE'S STORMS

JUSTIN KENDRICK

DAVID C COOK

transforming lives together

HOW TO QUIET A HURRICANE
Published by David C Cook
4050 Lee Vance Drive
Colorado Springs, CO 80918 U.S.A.

Integrity Music Limited, a Division of David C Cook
Brighton, East Sussex BN1 2RE, England

DAVID C COOK® and related marks are registered trademarks of David C Cook.

The website addresses recommended throughout this book are offered as a
resource to you. These websites are not intended in any way to be or imply an
endorsement on the part of David C Cook, nor do we vouch for their content.

Unless otherwise noted, all Scripture quotations are taken from the Holy Bible,
New International Version®, NIV®. Copyright © 1973, 2011 by Biblica, Inc.™ Used
by permission of Zondervan. All rights reserved worldwide. www.zondervan.com.
The "NIV" and "New International Version" are trademarks registered in the United
States Patent and Trademark Office by Biblica, Inc.™ Scripture quotations marked ESV
are taken from the ESV® Bible (The Holy Bible, English Standard Version®), copyright
© 2001 by Crossway, a publishing ministry of Good News Publishers. Used by
permission. All rights reserved. Scripture quotations marked NKJV are taken from the
New King James Version®. Copyright © 1982 by Thomas Nelson. Used by permission.
All rights reserved. Scripture quotations marked NLT are taken from the Holy Bible,
New Living Translation, copyright © 1996, 2015 by Tyndale House Foundation.
Used by permission of Tyndale House Publishers, Carol Stream, Illinois 60188. All
rights reserved. The author has added italics to Scripture quotations for emphasis.

Library of Congress Control Number 2024938433
ISBN 978-0-8307-8701-2
eISBN 978-0-8307-8702-9

© 2024 Justin Kendrick
Published in association with The Bindery Agency, www.TheBinderyAgency.com.

The Team: Michael Covington, Jeff Gerke, Justin Claypool,
Brian Mellema, Jack Campbell, Susan Murdock
Cover Design: James Hershberger
Author Bio Photo: Ian Christmann

Printed in the United States of America
First Edition 2024

1 2 3 4 5 6 7 8 9 10

060624

CONTENTS

INTRODUCTION

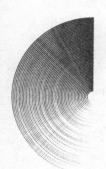

I experienced the love of God for the first time as a teenage kid. Before that first experience, I don't remember ever looking for God, but once I personally encountered his love, I couldn't stop pursuing him. I started devouring any book I could get my hands on that might help me understand him more. The first Christian book I ever read was given to me by my dad. It was called *Power for Living*, and it told stories about famous people who had experienced the love of Christ.

I can't remember many of the stories from the book, and I'm not even sure I ever finished reading it, but there was something about the title that has stuck with me all these years. *Power for Living*. Isn't that what we are all looking for? It wasn't called *Power for Existing*, because none of us want to just exist through life. We want to live. *Really* live. We want to make a mark, overcome our fears, and find fulfillment. We want to be happy and whole. The title sums up so many of our highest ambitions and suggests that life doesn't need to be lived from a place of weakness or frailty. You can overcome. You can live life *strong*.

But things haven't exactly gone the way we planned. An honest survey of our current cultural moment reveals that, for so many people, life is missing the mark. We've increased our comforts, advanced our technology, and created an endless assortment of entertainment options, but instead of finding deep personal fulfillment, most of us struggle to make it through the day.

Depression and anxiety continue to rise.[1] Fear about the future and insecurity about our own value and worth dominate our inner world. Instead of being happier, it seems that many of us are getting angrier and emptier. We told ourselves that with an assortment of options and enough autonomy we would finally be happy, but the wager hasn't paid off. Scholar Thomas Howard noted, "To our chagrin, we discover that the declaration of autonomy has issued not in a race of free, masterly men, but rather in a race that can be described by its poets and dramatists only as bored, vexed, frantic, embittered, and sniffling."[2]

Instead of being happier, many of us are getting angrier and emptier. We told ourselves that with an assortment of options and enough autonomy we would finally be happy, but the wager hasn't paid off.

Have you wrestled with an aching sense of vexation or boredom? Have you struggled under the pressure of a frantic pace? What's gone wrong in a world where we seem to have it all and at the same time still not have what we need most? Many people today lack a clarifying vision or direction for life, and it doesn't take a sociological expert to see that our world is moving closer to the edge of a cliff. How long can we hide behind Netflix subscriptions and prescription medications? How long can we blame everyone else for something that is broken *in* us? We need power for living.

Maybe the most concerning observation of all is the profound *fragility* that has come to define an entire generation. Simply put, we don't know how to take a hit. We've become obsessed with issues like work-life balance and limited hours at the office, and these things have their merit, but our focus on them is not because our jobs suddenly became more difficult. It's because our inner world is so fragile. When something goes wrong or circumstances throw us a curveball, we spiral out of control.

Most people are not living with a functional inner framework that can handle the pressures and problems of life, and the faith traditions of previous generations rarely play a central role in how we process life's challenges. Our convictions often lack depth and girth, and because they haven't been seriously tested, our inner lives remain in the shallow end of the pool. These words of Jesus have never been more relevant: "The thief comes only to steal and kill and destroy; I have come that they may have *life*, and have it to the full" (John 10:10).

How do we experience the fullness of life, and how do we avoid the traps of the thief? How can followers of Christ today deepen our convictions and call upon them in times of difficulty and struggle?

This book will explore the topic of Christian endurance and the promise found throughout the Bible of a life marked by supernatural power. In chapter 1, we will set the stage and consider God's invitation to a different way of life. From there, we'll learn how weakness is the starting point for spiritual strength and how all inner endurance comes from an understanding of God's love.

In chapters 4, 5, and 6, we will explore different aspects of spiritual stability, learning to apply God's promises and interact with him as our provider and protector. The last four chapters of the book are dedicated to moving beyond survival and into a life of victory and joy.

In these pages, you won't find "the ten steps to Christian endurance" or "the five ways to stop worrying." Although these things may sound helpful, real spiritual endurance is rarely tidy or linear. Life is unpredictable. We don't need ten steps—we need a Swiss Army knife. We need one tool that can serve us in a thousand situations, enabling us to overcome the challenges we face. That's why I've chosen to focus every chapter on the same centering goal: *grow faith*.

Faith is that deep "inner knowing" that can propel you through any trial. It's more than an intellectual conviction or an emotional experience, and it's strengthened every time we seriously reflect on God's truth and apply it to the issues swirling in our lives. Whenever faith gets stronger, deeper, or wider, endurance increases. With every chapter, you will be invited into a deeper understanding of your faith in Christ. It is my hope that the compound effect will be an inner life that can endure anything.

CHAPTER 1
ADJUSTING EXPECTATIONS
How God expects us to live

"A furious squall came up, and the waves broke
over the boat, so that it was nearly swamped."

Mark 4:37

It was just another normal day for sixteen-year-old Zac Clark. He was helping his mom with some chores in the yard at their home in Bellville, Ohio, when, in an instant, everything changed. Zac heard a cry coming from his neighbor's driveway, and when he rushed over to see what was wrong, he found his neighbor pinned underneath the man's car. The car jack had somehow slid out, and now the weight of the vehicle was crushing his neighbor's chest.

Zac didn't have time to think. Instead, he reached down, grabbed the underbelly of the car, and started to lift. Sixteen-year-old boys can't normally pick up cars, but in this moment, something inexplicable took place: Zac raised the three thousand-pound metal frame off his neighbor's chest, and when the pressure released, the man was able to move. Everyone was safe, tragedy was avoided, and Zac was suddenly a superhero.

It didn't take long for news outlets across the nation to celebrate the story of Zac's heroism.[1] How did he do it? Where did he find that kind of power? Although this event was certainly incredible, it's not an uncommon tale. History is full of moments when seemingly normal people perform feats of strength beyond rational calculation.

Men have run into burning buildings to save strangers. Mothers have rescued their children against impossible odds. For generations, we have told and retold the stories of heroes who saved lives, defied probability, and performed acts of extreme courage. It's a theme that finds its way into nearly all of our biggest movies and TV shows: an average person faces insurmountable odds and somehow finds a way to overcome.

These stories capture our imagination and resonate so deeply because they awaken within us the possibility of normal people possessing incredible strength. And deep down, we don't just want to read about it—we want to *do* it. We want to be the one who picks up the car and saves the neighbor. We want to be the one who doesn't fall apart when things get tough. Whether we recognize it or not, there is something in all of us that desires to be a person who comes through.

When I was a kid, my parents bought me a karate suit with a black belt. I never took a single martial arts lesson, but when I wore that suit, I felt powerful. I reasoned that I could kick through a wall as long as I had my suit on. I loved the feeling so much that I wouldn't take it off. My parents had to pin me down just so they could wash it. I resisted because, in my mind, taking off the suit meant transforming back into a normal kid.

I bet if you think about your childhood, you probably had something like a karate suit too. Maybe for you it was a Batman mask, or a princess crown, or a LeBron jersey, but whatever it was, you held to it tightly.

Peter Parker was a normal kid until he became Spider-Man. Adonis Johnson was an average boxer until he put on his father's boxing trunks and learned that his real name was Adonis Creed. Rey Skywalker left her desert planet and followed the Resistance across the universe, but she found herself in the process. Untapped potential. Undiscovered power. We retell the same story with a thousand subtle variations, but we love it every time because it calls us back to that deep inner desire. Average people can become strong.

But what happens when we take the karate suit off? What happens if we can't lift the car? Eventually, every one of us is confronted with the uncomfortable reality that we are not as strong as we want to be. Remember the time you buckled under the pressure? Remember when you were controlled by your anxieties and insecurities? Remember when you couldn't stand up to your boss? Remember when you didn't resist the temptation? Remember when you got scared and your fear caused you to cower and hide?

> **Eventually, every one of us is confronted with the uncomfortable reality that we are not as strong as we want to be.**

An honest assessment of the evidence will lead us to conclude that we are frequently too weak, too selfish, too tired, too frightened, or too busy to exhibit a strength that saves the day. Where then should we turn when troubles and trials come? If we can't consistently find the strength from within, is there any hope to endure?

The Other Side

The gospel of Mark tells the story of a moment of testing between Jesus and his disciples. Jesus had just spent the day teaching a crowd of people on the shore of the Sea of Galilee. When the sermon was over, he said to his disciples, "Let us go across to the other side" (Mark 4:35 ESV).

This invitation has always captured my imagination. In the most practical sense, Jesus was just inviting his followers to come with him across the lake. But in a broader sense, his invitation applies to all followers of Christ. He is forever leading us to the other side. He is committed to taking us further on our journey with him. In this sense, Mark 4 presents a compelling metaphor of the spiritual life, and it doesn't take much imagination for each of us to see ourselves in his boat.

Where is Jesus leading you? Where in your life do you need to cross over to the other side? Maybe right now you need to get on the other side of your doubts. They've held you back from fully trusting God, and your spiritual life has lacked depth and strength. You've sensed his inner call, but something inside you has been hesitant to respond. Or maybe you need to get on the other side of fragility. Circumstances have worn you down and you've found yourself cracking under the pressure.

The invitation to go with Jesus to the other side is so compelling because we find in it a spark of hope. If he calls you to the other side, it means you don't have to stay trapped in your dysfunction. It means you *can* change. You can live with a peace that surpasses understanding (Phil. 4:7), a joy that goes beyond words (1 Pet. 1:8), and a hope that endures any trial (Rom. 15:13). The apostle Paul wrote, "In all these things we are more than conquerors through him who loved us" (Rom. 8:37). This is a glimpse into the Christian life, which was always intended to be one that crosses over to the other side, the side of power and victory.

As soon as the disciples entered the boat with Jesus, the story took an unexpected turn. "A furious squall came up, and the waves broke over the boat, so that it was nearly swamped" (Mark 4:37). The Sea of Galilee is notorious for violent storms that seem to come out of nowhere, and on this particular night, things quickly went from bad to worse. The wind picked up, and the rain started coming down in sheets. This was no ordinary storm. The phrase translated "furious squall" literally means "a hurricane whirlwind."[2] The disciples found themselves in the middle of a hurricane, and it didn't take long for panic to set in.

Have you ever lived through a hurricane? As a young man, I served in relief efforts after Hurricane Katrina in 2005, and my volunteer team arrived on the scene just days after the storm had passed. I saw a thirty-foot RV that the storm had flipped upside down as if it were a Matchbox car, and I cleaned out houses that were buried in ten feet of mud. All of our cleanup work stopped when human body parts started washing up on the shore by our camp.

A hurricane should not be treated lightly, and the worst possible place to be when a storm like this touches down is in a tiny boat in the middle of a lake.

Throughout the Bible, a storm frequently serves as a symbol of the trials and troubles of life. Hurricanes come to us in the forms of unexpected tragedy, unforeseen loss, and unwarranted betrayal. "In this world you will have trouble" (John 16:33), Jesus said, and sometimes the trouble will arrive out of nowhere and descend upon us like a sudden storm.

Maybe things were going great for you until the phone rang and you learned about the car accident. Life felt safe until the doctor reviewed your scans and told you the news. No matter how stable and steady life might appear, we are all just one moment away from a hurricane. There are physical challenges like illness and severe injury, and there are internal challenges like fears and irrational thoughts. Some days you might wake up feeling depressed with no real explanation as to why.

Hurricanes in your mind. Hurricanes in your heart. Hurricanes in your marriage or with your kids. Where do they come from and, better question, how do we endure?

I imagine that the first reaction of the disciples was to try to solve the problem themselves, as most of us would do. Row harder. Put your back into it. But it didn't take long before they were exhausted. Confronted by their own weakness, they turned to Jesus, and to their surprise, they found their master cuddled up in a corner of the boat, asleep on a cushion (Mark 4:38).

How could Jesus be sleeping? Why would the Son of God, who perfectly represents the heart of the Father, doze off at this critical moment? The terrified disciples quickly jumped to the conclusion that Jesus must not care about them or their situation. "Teacher, don't you care if we drown?" (Mark 4:38).

Their reaction provides a glimpse into our own hearts. When we face circumstances that seem unfair, inexplicable, or beyond our strength, something in us is prone to question God. How could he let this happen? Doesn't he care? If he does, then why won't he do something? Like the disciples, we can quickly conclude that because Jesus doesn't immediately stop the storms we face, it means he is either not as loving or not as powerful as the Bible claims. But what if this hurricane nap is intended to model for us a different way of life?

While the disciples were panicking, Jesus was resting. They were drowning in feelings of terror, but he was perfectly at peace. He rests in the hurricane as a vivid picture of a better way to live, showing us that God doesn't always take away the storm, but he always gives us what we need to get through it. He views all of life from the perspective of eternity, and that perspective changes everything.

Which image more accurately expresses your approach to the hurricanes of life? Are you like the disciples, stressing and strategizing as you fight off anxiety, or are you more like Jesus, resting and reclining as the rain pours down? As unrealistic as it might sound, if you were convinced that it was actually possible to sleep through the storms, wouldn't you want to learn how?

Talking to the Weather

The disciples woke Jesus from his nap, and it didn't take long before he surprised them again. "He got up, rebuked the wind and said to the waves, 'Quiet! Be still!' Then the wind died down and it was completely calm" (Mark 4:39).

Try to imagine what these twelve followers of Jesus were feeling as they heard their rabbi *talk* to the weather. He yelled at the storm like a man yells at his dog, and the storm quickly submitted to its master. Jewish tradition taught that only God could command the weather.[3] People in the ancient Near East saw the sea as the great uncontrollable force, and Israel's understanding of God was largely shaped by his ability to dictate terms to the waters. God parted the Red Sea in order to deliver his people from bondage in Egypt, and he moved the Jordan River out of the way when his people needed access into the Promised Land. Some scholars have even suggested that mastery of the seas was "the basic idea of Israelite religion."[4]

Who is God? According to the Bible, he is the one who commands and controls the most chaotic sea. "Who has the wisdom to count the clouds? Who can tip over the water jars of the heavens?" (Job 38:37). The answer is clear: only God can do that. The story in Mark 4 is thematically connected to Psalm 107, where the psalmist described sailors who were trapped in a storm. In their terror, they cried out to the Lord.

> He stilled the storm to a whisper;
>   the waves of the sea were hushed.
> They were glad when it grew calm,
>   and he guided them to their desired haven.
> Let them give thanks to the LORD for his
>   *unfailing love*
> and his wonderful deeds for mankind.
>   (Ps. 107:29–31)

Calming the storm is a plain demonstration of God's *unfailing love*. The Hebrew word used here is *hesed*, which shows up over 250 times throughout the Old Testament. It describes the loyal, faithful, unwavering, covenant love of God.

The disciples in the boat knew Psalm 107. It was why they were so stunned by the actions of Jesus: calming the storm didn't just save their lives; it also put him on par with God. Jesus's demonstration of power was a revelation of his identity. He was not just a carpenter who came to teach Israel. He is God, come to save—the ultimate demonstration of *hesed*. Jesus is God's loving solution to our most dangerous storms.

But it's in this moment, after Jesus calmed the sea, when we reach the unexpected climax of the story. "He said to his disciples, 'Why are you so afraid? Do you still have no faith?'" (Mark 4:40). What exactly was Jesus driving at? He was clearly disappointed by their lack of trust, but what did he actually expect them to do? There can only be one explanation.

Jesus expected his followers to overcome their fears and respond to the storm with radical trust in God. They were still trapped in the natural, but he was driven by the supernatural. They were chained to the practical, but he was living with the certain knowledge that the kingdom of God was already breaking into the world. Jesus didn't just want to quiet the hurricane for them. He wanted them to learn for themselves. He wanted *them* to quiet the hurricane.

At first, this might sound ridiculous. After all, the disciples were just ordinary people. They were flawed and fragile like us. How could they stand up to a storm? It wasn't long after this storm-stopping experience that Jesus prepared them for his departure by saying, "Very truly I tell you, whoever believes in me will do the works I have been doing, and they will do even greater things than these, because I am going to the Father" (John 14:12).

If these words don't make you at least a little uncomfortable, then you haven't taken them seriously. His expectation is that *you can operate in the power of God*—and these two examples are not the only times we find this theme in the Bible. The prophet Isaiah made an outrageous claim when he wrote:

> Do you not know?
>   Have you not heard?
> The LORD is the everlasting God,
>   the Creator of the ends of the earth.
> He will not grow tired or weary,
>   and his understanding no one can fathom.
> He *gives strength* to the weary
>   and *increases the power* of the weak.
>   (Isa. 40:28–29)

Are you weak? Are you weary? In this text, God clearly offers his power to his people, but it seems that many of his followers haven't heard or just don't know what's available. We're doing life without the strength of God, when according to Isaiah, his strength—the same strength that holds the earth in place, keeps the planets in motion, and sustains all living things—is available to us.

When the apostle Paul prayed for the church of Colossae, he specifically mentioned this capacity for supernatural strength. "We have not ceased to pray for you, asking that you may be filled with the knowledge of his will ... being strengthened with *all power*, according to his glorious might, for *all* endurance and patience with joy" (Col. 1:9, 11 ESV).

Notice how Paul connected the idea of God's will for your life with God's power in your life. To fulfill God's will, you must learn to walk in God's power. He then said that these two ideas are largely dependent on *knowledge*. The follower of Jesus must know what God has made available before he is to access power beyond himself.

The power of God in our lives results in *all endurance*, and as the believer's capacity expands, so his attitude changes. Joyful patience marks his life. What used to frustrate him no longer does. What once caused anxiety now leaves him unfazed. It's obvious that Paul prayed this bold prayer from the conviction that this type of power is actually possible to obtain.

Just like Jesus in the boat, Paul believed that you can quiet a hurricane. You can operate in the power of God, and you can endure more than you ever thought possible through God's strength in you. But for this idea to become a reality, you must have the eyes of your heart opened so that you might know the "immeasurable greatness of his power toward us who believe" (Eph. 1:19 ESV). You have to see it. You have to know it. Do you?

There will be times in life when you lack physical strength. In the Old Testament, David cried out to God to increase his physical capacity, and God responded to his request. David testified that "with your help I can advance against a troop; with my God I can scale a wall" (Ps. 18:29). "He trains my hands for battle; my arms can bend a bow of bronze" (Ps. 18:34). Physical strength from God was imparted to David when he learned to access God's promise of power.

The prophet Daniel lacked understanding, and when he turned to God for help, God answered his prayer with supernatural knowledge, leading Daniel to exclaim, "Praise be to the name of God.... He gives wisdom to the wise and knowledge to the discerning. He reveals deep and hidden things" (Dan. 2:20–22).

The psalmist found that "on the day I called, you answered me; my *strength of soul* you increased" (Ps. 138:3 ESV). "My flesh and my heart may fail, but God *is the strength of my heart* and my portion forever" (Ps. 73:26). Physical strength, supernatural knowledge, and even emotional stability—the Bible is full of examples of God bestowing all three. It is impossible to honestly read the Scripture and miss God's expectation of a supernatural life. You were created to live a life of power *from* his strength.

Strangely, in our modern times, many Christians haven't taken these promises seriously. We've learned to rely solely on natural solutions to face the big storms in life, quickly turning to a new medication, physical fitness, or psychological therapy. We trust our own feelings and make our own plans. God uses all of these things to strengthen us at different times and in different ways, but there is often something missing at the center of our approach: we don't look to him as our primary source of power, and we haven't learned how to receive the power he has promised.

> **It is impossible to honestly read the Scripture and miss God's expectation of a supernatural life. You were created to live a life of power *from* his strength.**

It doesn't take long before the hurricane becomes too strong and we find ourselves drowning under the pressure, worry, or anxiety. We often end up managing the trials of life through the same strategies used by those who don't have Christ at all. We turn to entertainment to distract us from our problems or self-medicate to avoid our deepest feelings.

But what if life didn't have to be this way? What if there really was a way to overcome the storm and endure the trial with joy?

The Great Question

After Jesus calmed the storm, the disciples found themselves in a moment of internal crisis. They had no inner framework to process what they had just witnessed, and they were confused, terrified, grateful, and joyful all at the same time. The story ends with the disciples asking the question, *"Who is this?"* (Mark 4:41).

This question is the central point of the story. It serves as the doorway to faith[5] and the entry point into a life marked by the power of God. The right answer to this question leads us into the experiential reality of God's supernatural capacity.

Who is Jesus? Do you know him personally? Do you see him for all that he is and deeply understand what he has done for you? The premise of this book is that if we can more accurately answer the question of Mark 4:41, we can find the strength that God supplies. With a correct answer to this central question, we can learn to sleep through the loudest storms ... and even speak to hurricanes.

Before the disciples ever got into the boat, Jesus had already invited them to the other side. He doesn't invite us to cross over and then leave us in the middle of the storm. As we will see in the following chapters, sometimes Jesus removes the storm with a word, and other times he allows the storm for a season. Either way, just as he brought the disciples safely to the other side, so he intends to always see you through as well.

You can settle for a life of fear, or you can learn the secrets of a life of faith. You can pretend that the hurricane will never come, or you can prepare for the hurricane before it comes. If you want to take steps forward in the life of faith, it begins by adjusting your expectations. In this world you will have trouble. But take heart. Jesus has overcome the world, and his power now lives in you (John 16:33).

> *God moves in a mysterious way*
> *His wonders to perform;*
> *He plants his footsteps in the sea*
> *And rides upon the storm....*
>
> *Ye fearful saints, fresh courage take;*
> *The clouds you so much dread*
> *Are big with mercy and shall break*
> *In blessings on your head.*[6]

CHAPTER 2

THE WEAKNESS PARADOX
Embracing the truth about ourselves

"When I am weak, then I am strong."

2 Corinthians 12:10

Pablo Valencia got lost in the desert. He was searching for a hidden gold mine that he hoped would bring him riches beyond his wildest dreams, but when he and his companion ran out of water, they decided to split up. Now completely alone, Valencia found himself wandering across the Sonoran Desert, hoping for a miracle. The temperature hovered around one hundred degrees without a cloud in the sky. He drank his own urine. He sucked the liquids out of a scorpion. This was a desperate situation.

Research suggests that for a healthy man traveling through the desert without water, the expected time of survival hovers right around sixteen hours.[1] Valencia made it a full day, then two days, then three. Six days after Pablo Valencia's last sip of water, he was rescued, surviving nine times longer than expected, but his body told the story.

> His lips had disappeared as if amputated, leaving low edges of blackened tissue; his teeth and gums projected like those of a skinned animal, but the flesh was as black and dry as a hank of jerky; his nose was

withered and shrunken to half its length; his eyes
were set in a winkless stare, with surrounding skin
so contracted as to expose the conjunctiva, itself as
black as the gums.[2]

Pablo Valencia looked like a walking corpse, and he had traveled
over one hundred miles on foot through the desert. *One hundred miles
without water.* Most of us would struggle to walk ten miles in perfectly
cool weather with an endless supply of Gatorade, but he survived by
sucking on scorpion juice. Once his story got out, wherever he went,
people wanted to shake Pablo Valencia's hand, and for the rest of his
life he was treated as the living embodiment of *resilience.*

What does it really mean to be resilient? Resilience is the ability
to get crushed, stretched, or squashed, and still continue forward. In
my closet I have an old pair of work boots. I've used them for years,
yet they are not showing any significant signs of deterioration. They're
waterproof and weatherproof, and they were worth the money I spent
on them, because they've taken a beating and remained intact. That's
what I think of when I hear the word *resilient.*

The American Psychological Association tells us that resilience is
the process of adapting well in the face of adversity, trauma, tragedy,
or threats.[3] Resilient people are flexible and durable. They adjust to
the circumstances while at the same time maintaining an unshakable inner core. Professor of Psychology Angela Duckworth calls this
unique quality *grit.*[4] Grit, according to Duckworth, is the combination of passion and perseverance. It enables some people to keep going
when everyone else has given up.

In the movie *True Grit*, the character Rooster Cogburn embodies resilience like few others. He's a US marshal in the old American frontier, and he's hired by a young girl to chase down the man who killed her father and bring him to justice. Cogburn gets shot, stabbed, and thrown off a cliff, but nothing seems to slow him down. At one point he rides his horse through the night until the horse collapses under him. He then shoots the horse and continues on foot, all the way back to the town, where he saves the day.

Characters like Rooster Cogburn and Pablo Valencia don't seem to get the attention or accolades today that they once received from previous generations. Kids used to idolize men like this, but today we often consider their actions irresponsible, imbalanced, or unwise. We tend to prefer heroes who overcome with their wits more than their heart, and we celebrate people who find a way to avoid the hard work and still win the day. We want to do less and get more.

Ferris Bueller replaced Rooster Cogburn a long time ago, but the first time I saw the movie *True Grit*, I felt something stir inside me. Even in the middle of a culture that frequently undersells the importance of resilience, the inner impulse toward a resilient life still exists because God put it there, and until we learn to pursue it, we will always feel unfinished.

Jump over a Car

A few years ago, my brother-in-law got into a motorcycle accident. A car pulled out right in front of him, and he had to jump off his motorcycle and roll across the hood of the oncoming car. He landed hard on the pavement on the other side. He was rushed to the hospital, and after some tests, the doctor found that he hadn't broken any bones. He walked away with a few scrapes and cuts.

He was in great shape at the time of the accident, and at a follow-up appointment, the doctor told him that his muscles served like armor and protected him from serious injury. That's an encouraging diagnosis. Isn't that what you'd love to hear from your doctor? Your muscles are so big that you can jump over cars.

Right around the same time as his accident, I was playing basketball, and one of my friends accidentally smacked my hand. Right away, something didn't feel right. After a trip to the doctor, I learned that I had fractured a bone. I hadn't jumped off my motorcycle over a car to avoid disaster. Instead, I was just playing a friendly pickup game of basketball. The two contrasting experiences certainly got my attention, and I left the doctor that day feeling *less than* strong. One thought kept swirling around in my head: I was fragile.

I wish I could say that this was the only time in my life that I've felt fragile, but the more I've paid attention through the years, the more aware I've become of the feeling. A sense of fragility sometimes shows up in unexpected moments, and it has surprised me more than once. It has come to the surface when I'm impatient with my kids though they've done hardly anything wrong. It has appeared again when a friend lets me down and I can't move past the offense.

The schedule runs me ragged and I get a tightness in my chest. I'll struggle to take a deep breath. The pressures of the moment are too much. The frustration boils over.

When was the last time you experienced an overwhelming sense of your own weakness? What should we do in the moments when we come face to face with our limits? The most common response is to hide it. We learn to pretend that we are strong even when we're not, and we try to convince the people around us that we're fine. We fake it, stuff it, ignore it, or deny it. Maybe you were taught that real men don't cry or that if a woman shows emotion, it's a sign that she can't keep up.

The world we live in provides a thousand options for hiding. We can hide behind a drink or a pill. We can hide behind a TV show or a bag of Doritos. We use codependent relationships or important careers for camouflage, and we'll sometimes use money, attention, or the new toy in the garage to keep our weaknesses out of sight. Remember Adam and Eve in the Garden? As soon as sin crept into the equation, they found themselves hiding from God in the bushes (Gen. 3:8), and people have been perfecting the art of sewing fig leaves ever since.

Some people hide by taking it easy, acting like they don't really care about anything in life. Others hide by staying busy, unwilling to slow down and confront their own frailty. Eventually, bottled emotions explode, unsettled fears erupt, and what was once a small problem becomes a massive meltdown.

Author John Eldredge compared the horse to the camel to illustrate how different people deal with weakness. When pushed to their limits, horses slowly fade, but "camels are traitorous: they walk thousands of paces and never seem to tire. Then suddenly, they kneel and die."[5] I've found myself to be more of a camel. On the outside everything might look fine, until one day it all seems to collapse.

I experienced this phenomenon the week that my aunt died. I was holding her hand in the hospital, and I sat there in the chair next to her bed as her body went from warm to cold. She was in her early fifties, and our family was crushed. I went to the funeral on Friday, and I was back to work on Monday. One of my friends at work asked me how I was doing. I said I was doing *fine*.

That was a lie. I wasn't doing fine. But the most terrifying part was that I believed my own lie. I had convinced myself that I was fine, and when the hurricane of emotions swept through my life over the next days and weeks, I was caught completely off guard. If we don't recognize our own propensity to hide and actively fight against it, we will inevitably end up, as priest Henri Nouwen said, "living the whole of our life as one long defense against the reality of our condition."[6]

We can't hide our weakness forever, and when the veneer begins to crack and the truth starts to come through, many people immediately turn to *blaming*. Why are you so emotional? It's the way your parents treated you as a kid. Why are you failing at work? It's your boss's unrealistic expectations.

We tend to embrace a victim mentality before we consider self-examination, but rather than making us stronger, blaming others traps us in a cycle of self-deception. We start to believe our own stories, and the negative scripts we write require that we remain weak in order to justify the blame. When we reach this point, we are stuck.

Hide. Blame. Hide again. Blame someone else. Many people remain in this cycle their entire lives and never see the truth about themselves. Tragically, followers of Jesus fall into this trap just like everyone else. Consider the number of Christian leaders burning out, blowing up, or walking away from the church. One explanation for this trend is the pressure of ministry without the recognition of personal brokenness and weakness. Trying to be strong enough doesn't last forever, and when Christian leaders crumble, it testifies against the power that God promises to his people.

Beyond church leadership, church members are walking away from the faith in record numbers. They're giving up on the church, giving up on their marriages, and sometimes even giving up on God entirely. If you talk to those who have walked away, it doesn't take long before you recognize the story: Someone let them down. They couldn't handle the disappointment and decided that it was no longer worth the effort. They got tired. They got hurt. They snapped. But underneath these seemingly sudden moments of collapse, there is a much deeper issue, and until we confront it, we will never experience the strength to endure that God promises his people.

The Deep Flaw

In Romans 7, the apostle Paul seemed to be at war with himself. In just a few short lines, he gave one of the most accurate depictions of our fallen human condition. He wrote:

> I do not understand my own actions. For I do not do what I want, but I do the very thing I hate. Now if I do what I do not want, I agree with the law, that it is good. So now it is no longer I who do it, but sin that dwells within me. For I know that nothing good dwells in me, that is, in my flesh. For I have the desire to do what is right, but not the ability to carry it out. (Rom. 7:15–18 ESV)

Over the years, I've spent countless hours reflecting on this passage, and Paul's insights have dramatically reshaped my view of my own condition. Slowly and painfully, the truth in this text has pulled me out of hiding and blaming and forced me to see reality. Every time I think I've reached the bottom of this truth, I'm confronted with the fact that I've only scratched the surface.

If you've ever fought a battle with temptation, then these words resonate with you as well: *I don't understand myself.* I know it's stupid, but I find myself doing it. I know it's a lie, but I run to it anyway. I hate it, and I don't want it, and I vowed I'd never do it again, but something else lives in me that pulls me back in.

Paul's conclusion about himself is startling. *"I know that nothing good dwells in me,"* he wrote. At this point, many psychiatrists might interrupt the apostle. "Oh, now, Paul, don't be so hard on yourself," they would say. "You are a really good guy. Sure, you've got some troubles and flaws, but everyone makes mistakes."

How could Paul say that *nothing* good dwelled in him? He was a religious leader in his community. He had volunteered hundreds of hours and given away lots of money. To most people, it would seem that Paul was overstating the problem. What could he mean, and what does it have to do with overcoming our weaknesses?

To rightly understand Paul's words, we need to zoom out and see the larger narrative told in Scripture. In the story of creation, we learn that God bestowed on humanity his unique glory and image and crowned us with his honor (Gen. 1:27; Ps. 8:5). The purpose of our existence is to display the glory of God (Isa. 43:7), and the echo of his beauty can be heard in all the beautiful things that we create.

But the glory of humanity is only half the story. When sin entered the human race through the disobedience of our first parents, it distorted the image of God in all of us. Every single person has sinned and fallen short of God's glory (Rom. 3:23), and there is no one righteous before God, *not even one* (Rom. 3:10).

Many Christians have read these Bible verses and are quick to agree with them, but we often fail to internalize the deep truth that they teach. Sin has not added a few stains to our otherwise beautiful lives. We are not "basically good people" who just need to get a little better. We aren't even "bad people" who need to start being good. According to Scripture, we are dead people (Eph. 2:1), cut off from God and corrupt at our core. We might have physical life in our bodies, but we don't have eternal life in our hearts.

We carry within us a deep flaw, and it distorts every attempt at goodness and righteousness at the root. Every motive is flawed. Every good deed is at least partially polluted. We tell ourselves that we're helping a friend because we care about them, and we do, but we also care about being repaid or recognized for our good deed, and these mixed motives often remain hidden, even to us—until the repayment or recognition doesn't come.

> **We carry within us a deep flaw, and it distorts every attempt at goodness and righteousness at the root. Every motive is flawed. Every good deed is at least partially polluted.**

The book of Ecclesiastes articulates the human condition plainly: "The hearts of the children of man are *full* of evil, and *madness* is in their hearts while they live" (9:3 ESV). For many of us, this description feels like a gross overstatement. After all, you're not crazy, are you? You aren't Hitler or Stalin. How could the writers of Scripture claim that everyone is full of evil? Could it be that sin in you keeps you from seeing the sin in you?

"You will never make yourself feel that you are a sinner," explained Dr. Martyn Lloyd-Jones, "because there is a mechanism in you as a result of sin that will always be defending you against every accusation. We are all on very good terms with ourselves, and we can always put up a good case for ourselves."[7]

Sin itself blinds us from seeing the truth of our own condition, and this is why God has revealed the truth to us through his Word. Embracing the harsh reality of our own utter brokenness is the first step toward freedom and liberation, but until we understand this, we can't be free. Evil has found its way into every corner of our hearts, and this means that without God's direct intervention, every pure motive is tainted and every righteous ambition is polluted.

You might help an old woman cross the street because you care, but in a secret part of your heart, you also do it to be noticed by your neighbors. You might give the Salvation Army a donation to feed the poor, but you also do it to ease your own sense of guilt and bolster your sense of righteousness. The motives behind every action are layered, and hidden within those layers there is pride, lust, and greed.

To not know this about yourself is to remain deceived. You are a living tension, and nothing is pure. Within you there exists a sort of *madness*. Have you felt it? Have you identified it? One minute you're honest, but the next minute you're telling half the truth. One minute you're humble, but the next you're stoking your own ego. You look with pure eyes, but then you turn your head and look back with eyes of lust. This madness makes you fragile because you can't dig it out of your own heart. You can't *will* it away or work it away. You can't pray it away or hope it away.

Like Paul, you have the desire to do what is right, but you lack the ability to carry it out, and the deeper you look down the rabbit hole, the more you will see the hopelessness of your own condition. Underneath the good intentions, something dark has been lurking. Pastor and author Peter Scazzero called this your *shadow*. "Your shadow is the accumulation of untamed emotions, less-than-pure motives and thoughts that, while largely unconscious, strongly influence and shape your behaviors. It is the damaged but mostly hidden version of who you are."[8]

Have you recognized your constant thirst for attention? Did you notice the jealousy that sprung up when someone else was more successful than you? You lust when no one is watching. You're afraid of being found out. You work hard to prove to everyone that your life has value. Beneath the surface, your shadow deeply influences everything you do. The late laicized priest and author Brennan Manning wrote, "My false self staggers into each day with an insatiable appetite for affirmation."[9] Affirm me. Celebrate me. Notice me. It's never enough.

To see our shadow is devastating. It undercuts all our excuses and forces us to the end of ourselves. We can't fix it. We can't change it. Each of us stands guilty before God, and how we feel it. This is when the gospel finally begins to make sense. It's when we start to see that salvation is beyond what we could ever perform. It must depend on God alone. Paul believed that "nothing good" dwelled in him, and he was the greatest apostle who ever lived. Where does that leave the rest of us? It leaves us with only one option: *to collapse in the arms of Jesus.*

"What a wretched man I am! Who will rescue me from this body that is subject to death? Thanks be to God, who delivers me through Jesus Christ our Lord!" (Rom. 7:24–25).

Every person must come to the end of their own righteousness and face the truth. You are flawed and broken, and it's only by leaning into this painful reality that you are made whole. Pastor Dane Ortlund called this the "solid ground of self-despair." He wrote:

> When we see how desperately sick we are and pro
> foundly short we fall of the glory for which God
> intended us, we have already taken the first decisive
> step in bridging the vast gulf between who we are
> and who we were made to be.[10]

Healing comes through self-unraveling. Power comes through embracing weakness. These are among the great seemingly contradictory truths of the gospel. Only those who know they are blind can regain their sight, and only those who know they are weak can learn to move mountains.

Coming to Terms with Yourself

A few years ago, my wife and I took our first trip to Israel. While we were there, we visited the southern steps leading up the Temple Mount. As I walked up and down the stairs, I was struck by the fact that certain steps are a slightly different depth and width than others. It was easy to trip unless I kept my eyes down and watched where I was going. I learned later that the architecture of the staircase was intended to reinforce the right attitude in the traveler. No one should ascend the Temple Mount quickly. In order to avoid tripping, pilgrims had to keep their heads down and pay attention.

Intentional steps. Heads down. This is the only way we can enter the presence of God. It means no more posturing, proving, hiding, or blaming. It means that we confront our own shadows, and we acknowledge the inner madness. Finally, we collapse in the arms of Jesus. "Blessed are the poor in spirit, for theirs is the kingdom of heaven" (Matt. 5:3).

The person who sees himself as spiritually rich will leave God's presence empty-handed, and the person who sees himself as spiritually "middle class" will also miss out on the power of God. But the one who sees the truth of his own poverty, and even embraces it, to this one God entrusts *everything*. To him is the kingdom freely given.

Paul shared his journey of coming to terms with his own weakness in Romans 7, and he picked up this theme again in 2 Corinthians 12, describing his brokenness as "a thorn in the flesh." It's unclear exactly what he was referring to, and scholars have debated the point for generations, but whatever it was, Paul asked God for help. God, however, did not remove the thorn. Instead, he told Paul, "My grace is sufficient for you, for my power is made perfect in weakness" (2 Cor. 12:9).

The very thing that Paul thought was holding him back, God used to launch him forward. We tend to see our weakness and brokenness as disqualifiers, but God doesn't see it this way. To him, *weakness is the prerequisite.*

Remember Isaiah 40:29? It tells us that God increases the power of the *weak*. It never says that he increases the power of the strong.

We experience God's strength only to the degree that we internalize our own powerlessness. This is why he puts his glory in jars of clay (2 Cor. 4:7), because the unimpressive jar highlights his glory all the more. God allowed Paul to remain weak so that Christ might be seen as strong on Paul's behalf.[11]

> **We tend to see our weakness and brokenness as disqualifiers, but God doesn't see it this way. To him, *weakness is the prerequisite.***

God's plan to display his strength on the earth hinges on using *unqualified* people, and when we acknowledge our weakness, we become perfectly positioned for an outpouring of his power.

Very Dark, but Lovely

Have you come to terms with yourself? Have you looked down the rabbit hole and stared deep into your own weakness? My process of coming to terms with myself has been long and painful. I wish I could say that God dismantled my pride in an instant, but that hasn't been the case. For me, there have been numerous stops along the way, and the more progress I make, the more I see the need for greater change.

My first decade of full-time ministry was marked by energy and accomplishment. I pushed hard and achieved my goals. I was sure that my motives were pure, and I led from a place of painful ignorance when it came to my own shadow.

Then, about five years into planting our first church, things started to crack and splinter on the inside. The adrenaline that I mistook for faith was finally wearing off, and the grind of ministry was breaking me down.

One night, out of nowhere, I couldn't fall asleep. I tossed and turned for hours, and eventually I got out of bed and started work before the sun came up. The next night it happened again, and then again the night after that. As I lay in bed, my mind would spin. A week went by. An entire month passed. Something was wrong.

It seemed to me that this challenge came out of nowhere, but what I didn't realize was that the storm had been building for years. I had ignored my own weakness. I had avoided my own grief and had not been honest with myself.

The stress and pressure accumulated over time until they brought my life to a screeching halt. Finally, about five weeks into my struggle with sleeplessness, I hit a wall. I drove to work that morning, but when I tried to walk to the front door of my office, the whole world began to spin, and I collapsed. I found myself unable to get to the office door, so I embarrassingly crawled to my car and got back in the front seat. I sat there alone and started to weep.

For me, this moment marked a new level of my inner unveiling. My false self peered around the corner, and I caught a glimpse of my shadow. I saw that I was far more broken than I had ever imagined. I saw pride and fear and an unquenchable thirst for approval. I came face to face with my own insecurity. Somehow, all these enemies had remained hidden to me behind the walls of my life, but now they were coming into view for the first time. It was ugly, and I realized that it was only the beginning.

What should we do when we come face to face with our own weakness? Every natural impulse within us will tell us to hide or blame, but these tactics get us nowhere. Instead, we should collapse. We should let "the despair of who we are, left to ourselves, wash over us. In short, we die."[12]

After the day I couldn't walk to the office door, God began leading me into a new acceptance of my own frailty. I eventually ended up traveling to Montana for some time with a trusted friend where I could also find extended opportunities to be alone and make space for God. As I walked the trails at the base of the Blacktail Mountains, God patiently began introducing me to myself. I found comfort in the words of Psalm 51.

"Behold, I was brought forth in iniquity, and in sin did my mother conceive me. Behold, you delight in truth in the inward being, and you teach me wisdom in the secret heart" (Ps. 51:5–6 ESV).

To "behold" means "to gaze and to consider." You can't behold something in five minutes. It takes time and intentionality. In this psalm, the writer gazed upon the truth that from the day he was born, *iniquity* lived in his bones. Everything was tainted, and he could not save himself.

I began to see that I had lacked the deeper wisdom because I had resisted the truth about my own condition, and this was when the words of Paul came home to me: nothing good dwells in me. *Sin had left me broken beyond repair.* I acknowledged before God my own depravity, perversity, and frailty. Whereas *sin* speaks of wrong action, *iniquity* refers to a deeper brokenness in the unseen recesses of the heart. So I didn't just confess my sin—I also confessed iniquity.

"For you will not delight in sacrifice, or I would give it; you will not be pleased with a burnt offering. The sacrifices of God are a broken spirit; a broken and contrite heart, O God, you will not despise" (Ps. 51:16–17 ESV).

Psalm 51 is leading us to a place of honest surrender. God doesn't need our offerings. We can't pay him back as a punishment for our sins. Instead, he wants humility and a contrite heart, and when we bring him these things, something inside us begins to change. The jars of clay become vessels of honor. The weakness of man becomes the platform for God's strength to be revealed.

In the Song of Solomon, we read of two lovers who came together in marriage. The groom was head over heels for his bride, but the bride struggled to feel worthy of their union. She was a common girl, and he was a king. She stated in the beginning of the song, "I am very dark, but lovely" (Song 1:5 ESV).

In the culture of that time, darkened skin was a symbol of the lower class, since only the rich could afford to stay out of the sun. This woman's skin told the story of her humble upbringing, but even when the society at large said that she should be embarrassed by her dark skin, the love of her groom rewrote the story of her life.

The bride didn't deny the truth about who she was. "I am *very* dark," she said. But then she added a second observation that appeared to contradict the first. "Very dark, but—*lovely*." Through his love, she overcame the shame of her darkness. The love of the king had changed her, and she was now so inwardly secure that she was able to acknowledge her darkness and at the same time celebrate her acceptance. Her worth had been redefined by the king's embrace, and this experience made her both humble *and* confident.

Humble confidence. This is the defining mark of those who have encountered Jesus. This is the message that must bring us to the end of ourselves. Only those who recognize that they are incomplete can be made complete in Christ. Only those who know that they are spiritually dead can obtain resurrection life. "Those who exalt themselves will be humbled, and those who humble themselves will be exalted" (Matt. 23:12). This is the weakness paradox, and it serves as the great truth that leads us home.

CHAPTER 3

COMING HOME
The love of God and its implications

"May the Lord direct your hearts to the love
of God and to the steadfastness of Christ."

2 Thessalonians 3:5 (ESV)

Hiroo Onoda wouldn't come home. On December 26, 1944, he was sent to Lubang Island in the Philippines by the Imperial Japanese Army. Onoda served as a second lieutenant and was instructed to never surrender. When World War II ended with Japan's surrender in August of 1945, he could not believe the news. He concluded that the communication must have been enemy propaganda, so rather than going home, Onoda dug in.

Weeks went by, then months. Further communication confirmed that the war had ended, but Hiroo Onoda continued hiding, living off the land, and always preparing for battle. Eventually, an entire year passed. Then five years. Then a decade. This committed soldier would not leave his post.

Nearly thirty years after the war had ended, Japan sent Onoda's former commander, now a very old man, to convince the lieutenant to surrender. He traveled deep into the jungle, pleaded with Onoda, and finally convinced him to come home.[1] By this time, he had spent the best years of his life hiding and strategizing, fighting a war that was long over.

Some people called Hiroo Onoda a great war hero and celebrated his devotion and commitment to his country, but I think the story is more of a tragedy than anything else. For thirty years, he woke up every day believing a lie. He spent decades of his life in a battle that meant nothing. Who wants to fight an imaginary war? Who wants to struggle for a cause without a purpose? Hiroo Onoda wouldn't come home because deep down he was unwilling to *believe* the news.

Like the commander who wandered through the jungles of the Philippines looking for his lost lieutenant, Jesus came to seek and to save the lost (Luke 19:10). The message of the gospel is "the good news" that the great war against sin and death is decisively over. God has revealed himself to the world through the person of Jesus Christ. Through his life, Christ became our representative, and through his death he became our substitute. In resurrection, Jesus began the new creation and conquered death for all those who believe. Everyone who welcomes and embraces the good news is promised eternal life (John 3:16).

Strangely, something in the human heart tends to resist the message, and like Hiroo Onoda, we continue to fight a war that God has already declared to be over. We search for peace and fulfillment in other areas of life, or we quietly compile our record of good deeds to earn God's approval. Many people have interpreted the good news more like good advice, turning Christianity into a long list of dos and don'ts.

Probably the most famous story ever told about coming home is the story of the prodigal son. Jesus begins this parable by telling us,

"There was a man who had *two* sons" (Luke 15:11). In his book *The Prodigal God*, Tim Keller shows how these two sons provide a vivid picture of the two different ways we most often misunderstand the good news of the gospel.

The younger son leaves home and decides to do life on his own terms. His driving philosophy of personal fulfillment is self-discovery,[2] meaning that he plans to make all the rules for his life and choose what's right and wrong for him. He experiments with every pleasure that money can buy, but in the end, he finds himself empty, lonely, and starving. In an act of humility, the younger son returns home, and his father welcomes him back with open arms. His path teaches us that doing life on your own terms leads to a deep inner emptiness, but those who will humble themselves and come to God through Christ will find restoration and healing.

The second son mentioned in the story is the older brother. Although his role is sometimes overlooked, his approach to fulfillment in life can be even more deadly. Keller says that this brother operates from the life philosophy of moral conformity.[3] He assumes he can earn his father's love through good behavior. He always follows the rules, and he justifies himself by comparing his choices to the foolish choices of his younger brother.

When the father welcomes the irresponsible younger brother home, the older brother is furious. He won't enter the house or participate in the celebration because he doesn't think that his younger brother deserves the party. His path teaches us that moral conformity cannot lead to peace with God, since it avoids the truth of our own brokenness. By trying to earn our way to God, we deceive ourselves, and our self-righteousness keeps us from seeing the truth.

> Moral conformity cannot lead to peace with God. By trying to earn our way to God, we deceive ourselves, and our self-righteousness keeps us from seeing the truth.

Self-discovery will leave you empty, and moral conformity will leave you self-righteous. The parable of the prodigal son is intended to point us beyond these two unsatisfactory life philosophies and toward a radical third way to approach God. The third way does not come naturally. It shocks our system and surprises our rational minds. Most importantly, this third way carries within itself the power to change our hearts.

The Center of Life

When biblical writers refer to "the heart," they are not just talking about the emotional side of human nature. The *heart* is "the comprehensive term for the whole of our inner states, thoughts, feelings and will. It stands for the whole personality."[4] The heart is the center of life, and it follows that if the good news really is *good news*, then it must perform its primary work in the heart.

The apostle Paul provided a keen insight into the work of the gospel when he prayed, "May the Lord direct your hearts to the love of God and to the steadfastness of Christ" (2 Thess. 3:5 ESV). According to Paul, God must *direct* our hearts. The term used in this passage means "to make straight," and it was generally used to refer to ship captains, who were expected to make a straight course through the sea. The ocean, of course, has no paths or roads. It exists as one great expanse, and it was the unenviable job of the ship's captain to find a straight path and get the crew home.

In the same way, our hearts seek a way home, but we can't naturally find the path. Life is like an ocean, and all we can see is a vast expanse of endless waves. We need the Lord, our great captain, to direct our hearts home. But where are we headed? Where is the home of the heart?

Love. According to Paul, the heart's true home is the love of God. This is where the father sought to lead his two sons, and this is where God seeks to lead us. Minister and author Alexander Maclaren wrote that Paul's language in this text suggests a metaphor of the heart as "a great home with two chambers in it, of which the inner was entered from the outer."[5] The first room is the "love of God," and the second room is "the steadfastness of Christ."

Imagine a great house on the shores of the sea. You and I are lost amid the waves, but the Lord is the captain of the ship. He leads us through the sea to our home, and the first room we enter is the love of God. How do we know this love? We know it by the one who came to save us. God the Eternal Son became a man and entered the world on a rescue mission. Christ died for our sins, and through his sacrificial death he paid the debt of sin that we owed to God.

Remember in chapter 1 when we considered the story of Jesus calming the storm? The New Testament writer (Mark) used language to intentionally connect this story with the Old Testament story of Jonah.[6] In the story of Jonah, the storm subsided only after the prophet was thrown from the boat into the deep (Jon. 1:15). Jesus affirmed his connection with the story of Jonah when he called his three days in the grave "the sign of the prophet Jonah" (Matt. 12:38–41).

Jonah absorbed the ferocious storm by entering the sea, but Christ absorbed the storm of God's wrath toward sin by entering death for us. He calmed the seas that day on the boat with his disciples as a sign that pointed forward to the day when he would jump into the deep for us, giving his life so the raging sea would be stilled and we would have peace with God.

When the good news of what Christ has done is declared, God awakens those who receive it and transforms the heart. He removes the heart of stone that is dull toward him through sin and replaces it with a heart that is soft and responsive (Ezek. 36:26). This is the greatest miracle. Jesus called it the new birth, and Paul called it the new creation. God reaches down and turns the light on. He performs an invisible, miraculous inner change that results in a transformed life. What causes the change? The Holy Spirit causes the change through the spoken word of the good news of the gospel.

Renowned pastor and author A. W. Tozer described the new birth when he wrote, "To save us completely Christ must reverse the bent of our nature; He must plant a new principle within us so that our subsequent conduct will spring out of a desire to promote the honor of God and the good of our fellow men."[7]

How must we respond to this news? *Believe.* God loves the world so much that he gave his only Son. Whoever believes will not perish but have everlasting life (John 3:16). Believing the good news leads to the new birth, which changes the individual at the core. No longer are you a hell-bent sinner at the root. Although you still live in a sinful body, your inner self has been transformed and made alive. This was why Paul could write that nothing good dwelled in him—that is, in his *flesh.* The flesh will still rage against God, but because of the new birth, that is not your deepest self. By the mysterious, supernatural work of God's grace, you are a new creation.

The doctrine of justification states that through an instantaneous act of God, your debt of sin has been paid in full, and God has declared you blameless in his sight. Like a criminal who is declared "not guilty," you have been released from your debt through the shed blood of Jesus. You are justified by faith, and you now have peace with God (Rom. 5:1).

Justification is a gift that must be received, while sanctification is a progressive process that we participate in. The word *sanctification* describes the ongoing action of turning from sin and living in holiness. Sanctification is progressive as we work in partnership with God. Justification is instantaneous.

Through sanctification, God changes us *inside out*, as the Holy Spirit works in us day by day. Through justification, God changes us *outside in*, as the truth of his grace declares that we are blameless in his sight.[8] But the good news can almost become bad news if we don't understand the important relationship between justification and sanctification.

We often think that by trying harder we can overcome the flesh, and this leads to more frustration and failure. We try and try until we realize that we can't reach God's standards on our own. For some, this leads to despair, but for most, it leads to self-justification by comparison. We judge ourselves against the failures of others, and this allows us to prop ourselves up and overlook our own shortcomings. Like the older brother in the story of the prodigal son, we become entitled and self-righteous. We forget the truth of the weakness paradox.

When we try to change by our own strength, we've missed the essential relationship between justification and sanctification. *The only way to consistently grow in sanctification is to regularly feed it with the truth of justification.*

Stated differently, the only way to grow in holiness and obedi-ence to God is to remain in the truth of his undeserved love. You are accepted by God not because you perfectly obey. Rather, you learn to obey by believing that through Christ you are already perfectly accepted by God. You don't perform good deeds to justify your worth. Instead, you receive worth from God, who gave his Son because he thought saving you was worth it.

The heart's true home is the love of God, and when we receive his love, we are changed, and good deeds are the fruit. Brennan Manning wrote, "Define yourself radically as one beloved by God. This is the true self. Every other identity is illusion."[9]

> ## The only way to grow in holiness and obedience to God is to remain in the truth of his undeserved love.

Since God is the ultimate arbiter of reality, who are we to debate with him? If he says we are forgiven, accepted, blameless, and loved, then we have no right to project what we feel over what he has declared. His good news must *speak over* what we feel, and our hearts come home as we choose to make the reality of the gospel *more real* than our own thoughts and feelings.

That's why Paul's frustrations expressed in Romans 7 are sand-wiched between the higher realities of Romans 6 and 8. It's true that nothing good dwells in your flesh (7:18), but there is a higher truth:

"Just as Christ was raised from the dead by the glory of the Father, we too might walk in newness of life" (6:4 ESV). "In all these things we are more than conquerors through him who *loved* us" (8:37 ESV).

Because Jesus is alive, you can be sure that the good news is true. Because he loves you with an everlasting love, you can face any trial and overcome through him. How secure is God's love toward you? He speaks through the prophet Isaiah: "'Though the mountains be shaken and the hills be removed, yet my unfailing love for you will not be shaken nor my covenant of peace be removed,' says the LORD, who has compassion on you" (Isa. 54:10).

His love will never change. His gospel cannot be reversed. God can't go back on his commitment to love you, because through the new birth, Christ now dwells in your heart. This means that when God sees you, he sees his Son and he loves you *even as* he loves Christ (John 17:23). He doesn't just tolerate you. He isn't in heaven rolling his eyes in disgust or frustration. The eternal, undying love of the Father toward the Son—that same love—now and forever will remain aimed at you.

This is the gospel. Nothing can separate you. The tragedy of modern Christianity is that so many followers of Christ live more like Hiroo Onoda and less like the apostle Paul. If anyone had good reason to wallow in shame, it was Paul, who persecuted the church and murdered Christians before coming to faith in Christ. But instead of paying penance, Paul collapsed into grace and believed the good news.

Can the same be said of you? Has your life been radically redefined by the love of God? Has his love for you become the firm foundation of your identity and worth? What does it actually look like when a person is deeply, inwardly convinced that he is loved by God?

It looks like *stability*. Just as firmly planted trees are fed generously by their roots, so do those who plant themselves in the gospel discover an inner stability that impacts every area of life.

If Christian endurance begins with the weakness paradox, it comes home through the revelation of the love of God.

The Inner Room

"May the Lord direct your hearts to the love of God and to the steadfastness of Christ" (2 Thess. 3:5 ESV). The first chamber of the heart is the love of God, but there's another room that we are invited to enter. Paul called this inner chamber "the steadfastness of Christ," and it's here that we discover the next lesson in how to quiet a hurricane.

Notice the order of Paul's prayer. First comes the love of God, and then comes the steadfastness of Christ. This inner room of steadfastness can be accessed only *through* the outer room of love. The heart must first enter the love of God, and then from that sacred space, we can go deeper. Steadfastness is one of the central themes of the New Testament. It's translated "endurance" or "patience" in other contexts. It's describing something more than what Pablo Valencia had as he crossed the desert without water or what Rooster Cogburn had as he chased down outlaws. This endurance is greater than natural grit. It's supernatural power.

The phrase "the steadfastness of Christ" implies that Christians should seek to endure hardships just as Jesus endured. Jesus is our model, but he is far more than that. If this prayer meant only that we should follow the example of Jesus, then every Christian would find themselves trying harder but seeing little progress.

But Paul prayed that the Lord would direct us into the steadfastness of Christ because the very energy that propelled Christ out of the grave now lives in us. He is our source, and through the love of God, we access the *very strength* of Jesus. This means that you can be "strengthened with all power, according to *his* glorious might, for all endurance and patience with joy" (Col. 1:11 ESV). His might lives in you. The text could not be plainer, yet we hesitate to take it seriously. Let the truth sink in. You have access to the strength of Jesus.

Once you catch a glimpse of this promise, you realize that it's found all over the New Testament. The strength of Christ is not reserved for the most holy, studious, disciplined Christians. Instead, it's for the weak and incompetent, provided that we enter through the love of God. Grace makes you strong. Grace is, by definition, unearned and undeserved power from God.

"Be strengthened by the *grace* that is in Christ Jesus" (2 Tim. 2:1 ESV). "It is good for the heart to be strengthened by *grace*" (Heb. 13:9 ESV). When we try to conjure up the strength to endure difficult things through our own self-discipline or effort, we disrupt the flow of God's grace in our lives. But when we turn to God from a place of inner dependence and faith, the same power that brought Jesus up out of the grave is made available to us (Rom. 8:11). How can we learn to access this strength every day, moment by moment? That's the most exciting part. Just *look to him*.

Learning to Look

According to Paul's simple prayer, it's the Lord who directs our hearts to the love of God and the steadfastness of Christ (2 Thess. 3:5). Jesus is our Lord. He's the captain of the ship, the one steering our lives toward our heart's true home. Every day, he straightens the course another degree. Every day, he calls you to get your eyes off the waves and fix your gaze back on him. The ship functions best when the crew members keep their eyes on the captain.

In chapter 21 of the Old Testament book of Numbers, there is a strange story about the people of Israel. They were making their way across the desert to the Promised Land, and in the midst of their hardships in the wasteland, they began to grumble and complain. It was hot. They were tired. Food was limited. Water was scarce. The people blamed God for all their troubles.

Their complaints were answered by a new round of troubles: venomous snakes invaded the camp. People started dying from the snakebites, and as the panic spread, the Israelites realized that they had dishonored God and needed to repent. God heard their prayers and had mercy on the people, but his solution to save them from the snakes seemed to come out of nowhere.

> The LORD said to Moses, "Make a snake and put it up on a pole; anyone who is bitten can look at it and live." So Moses made a bronze snake and put it up on a pole. Then when anyone was bitten by a snake and looked at the bronze snake, they lived. (Num. 21:8–9)

Clearly, there were no medicinal benefits to looking at a bronze snake on a pole. In fact, of all the symbols that God could have chosen, this was the most unexpected. The serpent was a symbol of the curse. In the minds of the Jewish people at the time, especially as they were suffering from snakebites, serpents didn't save—they killed.

This story seemed to get little attention through the history of Israel, and it remained buried in the Old Testament archives until Jesus suddenly pulled it out as a prophetic symbol of the gospel. When the religious leader Nicodemus came to Jesus at night, Jesus told him that he must be born again. When Nicodemus responded with confusion about the new birth, Jesus referred to the story: "Just as Moses lifted up the snake in the wilderness, so the Son of Man must be lifted up, that everyone who believes may have eternal life in him" (John 3:14–15).

Jesus connected the snake in the desert to himself, informing us that it was a preview of the gospel. How could this be? Long before creation, sin, death, or suffering, God knew that he would send his Son to save the world, and hundreds of years before the Eternal Son took on flesh and blood, God told Moses to put a bronze snake on a pole.

The snake represents the curse. It was the snake who tempted Eve. It was the snake who brought sin into the world. Jesus connected himself with this image because on the cross he *became* the curse for us (Gal. 3:13). Paul wrote, "God made him who had no sin *to be sin* for us, so that in him we might become the righteousness of God" (2 Cor. 5:21).

In the Old Testament story, those who were bitten by the serpent only needed to *look*, and when they fixed their eyes on the snake, they were healed. In the same way, when we fix our eyes on Christ and see that he became the curse for us, we are healed. We are born again, given a new heart, and transferred from death to life. How does it happen? Just by looking. Dane Ortlund wrote, "The final conclusion, the deepest secret, to growing in Christ is this: look to him. Set your gaze upon him. Abide in him, hour by hour. Draw strength from his love."[10]

As we look to Christ, the love of God becomes real, and the strength of Christ becomes our own. God foretold his plan through the prophet Isaiah. "Look to Me, and be saved, all you ends of the earth! For I am God, and there is no other" (Isa. 45:22 NKJV). This is the way to access the power of Christ: *look and live.*

On a snowy January day in 1850, Charles Spurgeon felt an uncontrollable urge to go to church. He wasn't a Christian, and the snowstorm had shut down nearly every public gathering. Spurgeon went out anyway, and he found a small Methodist church that was open.

Only fifteen people sat in the pews, and the pastor was unable to attend because of the snow, so the local shoemaker got up to preach. He chose for his text Isaiah 45:22. The shoemaker explained that "looking" doesn't require a college education or a great deal of labor. You don't earn the ability to look. Any child can learn to do it. But *where* we look is of the utmost importance. "Look to *Me*, and be saved," the text declares.[11]

Our tendency is to look to God *plus*. We might look to God plus our efforts or God plus our good deeds. We might look to God plus our relationships or God plus our religion. But none of these other things saved the Israelites who were bitten by the snakes. They just looked to the bronze serpent on the pole, and when they did, they lived.

As Spurgeon heard this simple message, a light came on in his heart. He recounted:

> I saw at once the way of salvation. I know not what else he said—I did not take much notice of it—I was so possessed with that one thought. Like as when the brazen serpent was lifted up, the people only looked and were healed, so it was with me.... There and then

the cloud was gone, the darkness had rolled away,
and that moment I saw the sun.[12]

This is the gaze of the one who experiences the power of Jesus. Have you seen the sun? Have you understood the great gift of the gospel, and do you look to Christ alone? Look to him now. Set your hope on him. From this inner posture, his power comes to you.

On the day that Jesus rose from the dead, he appeared to two of his disciples on the road to Emmaus. They hadn't yet encountered the risen Christ, and when Jesus arrived, they didn't immediately recognize him. They were heartbroken and confused by the cross, and they couldn't understand why God would let him die.

The two disciples talked with Jesus their entire walk home, until he finally interrupted them and rebuked them for their dull, unbelieving hearts. "Beginning with Moses and all the Prophets, he interpreted to them in *all* the Scriptures the things concerning *himself*" (Luke 24:27 ESV).

Jesus led them through the stories of the Old Testament. Maybe he mentioned the bronze serpent in the wilderness or the covenant with Abraham, the ark that delivered Noah or the angel that met Daniel in the lions' den. Maybe he mentioned the prophecy of the suffering servant in Isaiah 53 or David's description of the crucified king in Psalm 22. We aren't given the details of their conversation, but we do know that Jesus used the stories of Israel's history to unveil the greater story of God's plan to save the world through the gospel of Christ. Their hearts burned within them as he spoke (Luke 24:32), because God was using these connections to wake them up.

In his providential wisdom, God placed clues, pictures, metaphors, and types throughout the Old Testament so that we could see Jesus more clearly today. How are we to understand a metaphor in the Bible? Minister Eugene Peterson defined a biblical metaphor as "a word that makes an organic connection from what you can see to what you can't see."[13]

Through these connections, the invisible truth of the gospel becomes tangible, and the theoretical concepts of grace become real. Christ *is* the bronze serpent lifted up on the pole, and when we see him in this light, knowing that God had this plan in mind all along, our faith grows stronger. We see the sun, and our hearts realize that the promises must be true. The gospel becomes good news *in* us.

You are loved by God, and with his word on your lips, you can learn to quiet a hurricane. The more your heart is convinced of the trustworthiness of God's Word, the more his power manifests in your life. The weakness paradox teaches us that before we can access the strength of God, we must come to terms with the truth about ourselves. Then, we come home to the love of God and the steadfastness of Christ and train our hearts to take him at his word.

CHAPTER 4

TAKE HIM AT HIS WORD
Restructuring your life around eternal promises

*"When the sun had gone down and it was
dark, behold, a smoking fire pot and a flaming
torch passed between these pieces."*

Genesis 15:17 (ESV)

"The city bus doesn't cost twenty dollars." Those words still ring in my ears even though it's been a long time since my friend said them. I was a teenage kid, eager to obey God and help people. One day while I was standing outside of church, a man I didn't know approached me and asked for help.

"I'm sorry to bother you," he said. "I lost my wallet and I need to get home. Do you have any money that I could use to catch the city bus?"

"I'd love to help," I said. "How much does the bus cost?"

"Twenty dollars."

I handed the man my last twenty-dollar bill. I didn't have much, but this guy needed to get home. He thanked me and immediately went on his way.

A few seconds later, my friend approached. "Hey, were you just talking with that guy?"

"Yeah, why?"

"Well, he's a drug addict, and he's been coming around here making up stories and asking people for money to pay for his addiction. Just make sure you don't give him any cash."

A wave of awkward embarrassment swept over me. My palms started to sweat. My face felt hot. My friend gave me a long stare. "Well," I explained, "this time he lost his wallet and needed money for the city bus." As the words came out of my mouth, I found myself wanting to pull them back in.

"How much did you give him?" he asked.

"Twenty dollars."

He chuckled. "The city bus doesn't cost twenty dollars. It costs *one* dollar."

I hadn't even considered how much the city bus might cost. That day, I accidently paid for a man to get high, and I still remember the feeling. I felt *small*. Foolish. No one likes to get tricked or be taken advantage of, and I walked away from that interaction determined to add a little wisdom and savvy to my compassion.

Trust is the currency of any relationship. It allows people to grow together, and without it you can't build anything significant. We all have "that person" in our lives whom we love but just can't trust. If love is like the glue that holds people together, then trust is like the brick that's used to build something great. Without trust, you might be glued, but you're not building.

A strong trust between two people usually grows slowly over time, brick by brick, through experience. Every time someone in a relationship comes through and proves their trustworthiness, trust has an opportunity to grow. Of course, lies, inconsistency, and unfaithfulness undermine trust and cause the structure of the relationship to crumble.

> **If love is like the glue that holds people together, then trust is like the brick that's used to build something great. Without trust, you might be glued, but you're not building.**

Recently, my three-year-old daughter woke up from her afternoon nap, and it was obvious that something was wrong. She told me, "Daddy, I don't want any *awigators* in my room." That seemed like a reasonable request to me. I realized that earlier that day my wife had taken our kids to the zoo, where my daughter had seen an alligator for the first time. Apparently, the alligators had paid her a visit in her dreams. I responded without even thinking. "Honey, *I promise* no alligators will get in your room." She trusted me, and that's been the last time we've talked about an awigator invasion.

This story oversimplifies the complex world of relational trust, but our relationship with God follows the same basic principle. In order to grow in a relationship with God, you must learn to trust him more. This is where things get a little complicated, because a relationship with God is not quite like any other relationship. God is invisible, he rarely speaks audibly, and sometimes it seems like he isn't there at all.

A trust relationship with God is especially challenging for another reason: he doesn't see the world the way we do, and his thoughts are light-years beyond the way we think. "As the heavens are higher than the earth, so are my ways higher than your ways and my thoughts than your thoughts" (Isa. 55:9).

Sometimes, God explains what he's doing and why he's doing it, but most of the time, he feels no obligation to explain himself. "Whatever the LORD pleases, he does" (Ps. 135:6 ESV). Does that verse make you a little uncomfortable? One reason for our discomfort is that we live in a world that has elevated our own reason and rational thinking to the very top of the social food chain. This means that most of us live with an unspoken assumption that we deserve answers, even from God.

For example, think of the last time you went to the doctor. Let's say the doctor and nurses performed a series of tests and then told you that they didn't know exactly what was wrong with you. When this happens, most of us aren't just disappointed—we're mildly offended, because something inside us assumes that there's a rational explanation for *everything*. We often project this expectation onto God, and when he refuses to provide adequate answers to our problems, *doubt* sneaks into the relationship.

The Problem of Doubt

Will God really do all that he says he will do? Is he good? Is he just? How can we be sure? The New Testament word for *doubt* means "to be divided in two." Imagine a person desperately trying to move in two directions at the same time. It's frantic and frustrating, and the result is a lot of motion but little progress.

Doubt can be a paralyzing experience, and it impacts everyone who seeks to grow in their relationship with God. If we don't address our doubts and process our doubts, they will eventually undermine the foundation of our faith. Are you sure that God really cares about you? Are you confident that he will come through for you when you need him most? Is he with you now? Is he *for* you? How can you be sure that God even exists?

For a lot of Christians, *doubt* seems to be treated like a dirty word. There appears to be an unspoken rule that Christians can't talk about their doubts, admit that they have doubts, or question any of the basic tenets of the faith. Many traditional cultures and Christians from previous generations have taught that doubt is *bad* and if you wrestle with doubt, then there must be something wrong with you. Because of this, doubt sometimes carries a stigma and shame with it. "Real Christians" don't ever second-guess God, do they?

Our doubts usually begin in the mind with a question or a problem, but they quickly seep down into the subterranean parts of our emotions. There are times when you won't even know what you're doubting, yet your faith and trust in God will feel handcuffed. Since many Christians have no outlet for their doubts, their confidence in God eventually crumbles under the pressure of unspoken uncertainties.

You probably know at least one or two people who considered themselves followers of Jesus until tragedy struck or trials came. As soon as these problems swept in, they lacked the internal framework to process their doubt. It wasn't long before they were ready to just give up on God and walk away. Doubt for a Christian can be a profoundly lonely place. Since we are taught that all doubt is "bad," the doubter finds himself hiding his questions, and this causes the questions to expand and fester even more.

If many traditional cultures have left us with the impression that all doubt is bad, then our modern secular culture often takes the opposite approach. We were told by Voltaire that certainty is absurd.[1] Shakespeare said that modest doubt is the beacon of the wise.[2] Over time it seems we've developed an intellectual snobbery that looks down on anyone who holds to deep convictions, and we assume that to be sure about anything is at best naive and at worst arrogant. Skepticism has strangely become a badge of honor, and this allows us to never commit to anything fully.

I'm sure you've heard people say things like "I think that every religion is basically the same. It would be arrogant to say that your religion is the only way to God. People should discover truth for themselves and find what's true for them."

Statements like this sound rational and humble in our current cultural context, but they are intellectually dishonest at their core. The person who holds to this conviction is saying that no one should make an exclusive truth claim, but they don't realize that their assertion that all religions are the same *is* an exclusive truth claim. They're doing the very thing that they claim no one should do. The skeptic is condemning absolute truth while at the same time treating their own convictions as absolute.

What we must understand is that to *not* believe in God *is* a statement of faith. Everyone must trust someone or something. There is no middle ground. We must wager our lives and our eternities on either one conviction or the other, and rather than seeing doubt as a bad thing, Christians must learn to see doubt as a natural part of growing faith.

Tim Keller wrote, "A faith without some doubts is like a human body without any antibodies in it.... A person's faith can collapse almost overnight if she has failed over the years to listen patiently to her own doubts, which should only be discarded after long reflection."[3]

If many Christians have wrongly hidden their doubts, and many non-Christians have hidden behind their doubts, what should we do when faced with questions and uncertainties about God? The Bible provides an intriguing alternative. Rather than hiding their doubts or ignoring their doubts, many of the Bible's biggest heroes openly processed their doubts with God and with community.

Remember Thomas? He's often remembered as "the doubting disciple," but Jesus never called him that. When the other disciples saw Christ risen from the dead, Thomas wasn't there, and he struggled to believe their testimony. Instead of isolating himself or disconnecting from his faith community, Thomas stayed and processed his doubts until Jesus appeared to him. Jesus didn't condemn or rebuke Thomas. He just gave him greater evidence to grow his trust (John 20:24–29), because Jesus is patient and compassionate with the doubter. This is how he met Thomas, and this is how he will meet you too.

Our inner tendency toward doubt shouldn't be a reason for shame or embarrassment, but we must also realize that not every doubt will be fully satisfied. Sometimes we assume that with enough evidence, all our doubts will disappear forever. We tell ourselves that if Jesus appeared to us in a dream or spoke to us with an audible voice, we'd never doubt again. But that's just not true. Contrary to our assumptions, great miracles won't permanently extinguish doubt.

In the gospel of Matthew, Jesus spoke with his disciples right before he ascended to heaven, commanding them to go into all the world. By this time in the story, the disciples had seen Jesus walk on water, heal the sick, and cast out demons. They had a massive archive of miraculous experiences to extinguish their doubts, and along with the past miracles, Jesus himself was standing in front of them, risen from the dead.

If ever there were a moment when human beings would be completely free of doubt, this should be it, but just before Jesus ascended into heaven, Matthew recorded that "when they saw him, they worshiped him; *but some doubted*" (Matt. 28:17). Even with great evidence, "some doubt" remains.

These words provide a stunning revelation of our true condition, teaching us that at its root, doubt is not rational. If it were, the evidence would have officially silenced their doubts, but it didn't. That's because, at its root, doubt is spiritual. Behind our doubt there is a cosmic spiritual battle, and we can't win the battle with rational tools alone. We can't explain away doubt or analyze our way out of unbelief. We must add spiritual weapons to our fight against doubt (2 Cor. 10:4), and this is why God's Word serves as an essential tool in the development of faith.

He Gave Us His Word

Paul explained the importance of Scripture when he wrote to Timothy:

> From infancy you have known the Holy Scriptures,
> which are able to make you wise for salvation through
> faith in Christ Jesus. All Scripture is God-breathed

and is useful for teaching, rebuking, correcting and training in righteousness, so that the servant of God may be thoroughly equipped for every good work. (2 Tim. 3:15–17)

Paul called the Scripture "God-breathed," and Peter said that the authors of the Bible spoke as they were "carried along by the Holy Spirit" (2 Pet. 1:21). Over four hundred times in the Old Testament, we find the phrase "thus says the Lord," and over 350 times we find the phrase "declares the Lord." In all these instances, the Bible is clearly claiming that the words written are to be understood as the very words of God.

Psalm 119 tells us that the unfolding of God's words brings light and imparts understanding (v. 130), and Isaiah tells us that God's word endures forever (40:8). When Jesus was tempted by the devil in the wilderness, he defeated every temptation with a quote from Scripture, teaching us that Jesus himself believed that the words recorded in the Bible carry power to push back darkness and overcome Satan. When you're tempted or tested, where do you turn? Is Scripture the first words on your lips, as it was for Jesus?

Some have suggested that the Bible is outdated. It was written thousands of years ago, after all, and society has changed so much since those days. It's true that culture has changed dramatically, but the human heart still wrestles with the same issues. The more we study the lives of David, Ruth, Moses, Jacob, Esther, and Peter, the more we recognize our struggles in their struggles. The revelation contained in the Bible has never been more relevant or more needed, since the human heart remains in desperate need of God.

Other critics throughout history have claimed that the Bible is oppressive because it commands people to do things that we might not naturally desire to do. We inwardly bristle at the idea of having an authority outside ourselves that rules over us. Our sinful nature inclines us to elevate autonomy as the highest freedom and individuality as a sacred right.

But the more you study the Scripture and understand the heart of God, the more you will discover that all of God's limits actually work to bring life. The cross of Jesus has perfectly revealed God's heart of love toward sinners, and as we grow in trust, we find that his limits don't rob us of freedom. They lead us to a better life and a higher freedom.

Many Christians hold to the idea of the Scripture as God's Word, but few actually treat the Bible with this level of reverence. We often compare what the Bible says to our own rational thinking and then pick and choose the parts we like. This robs Scripture of its power. If we take only the parts we are inclined to agree with and edit out the parts that offend us, we inevitably create a god in our own image. The result is self-worship disguised as God worship. If we don't believe in a God who can correct us, then we don't believe in God at all.

Real relationship with God requires growth in trust, and trust grows only when we take God at his word. The revelation of God contained in the Bible must become the foundation for our understanding of all of life. It must be allowed to confront us and contradict our way of thinking and then reshape us when necessary.

Paul warned Timothy that in this world, "evildoers and impostors will *go from bad to worse*, deceiving and being deceived" (2 Tim. 3:13). The language he used here suggests that culture is naturally regressive. It's always moving from one thing to the next. What was once rated R is now rated PG. What was once off limits is now acceptable. Sin, by its very nature, is moving us further and further from God.

> **If we edit out the parts of the Bible that offend us, we inevitably create a god in our own image. If we don't believe in a God who can correct us, then we don't believe in God at all.**

In contrast to the nature of this world, where truth changes and rules expand, the ways of God are fixed. "But as for you, *continue in what you have learned and have become convinced of*" (2 Tim. 3:14). Spiritual growth occurs in us not when we move on from the truth of God, but when we hold on more tightly to it, going deeper into the truth and applying it more fully.

As we saw in the last chapter, Jesus wants to guide us home by teaching us to remain in his love. Staying there leads to growth, healing, and life. Jude taught that we must learn to "keep ourselves in the love of God" (Jude 1:21 ESV). But when our minds are wrestling with doubts and our circumstances are overflowing with problems, remaining in a place of trust is not easy. Where do we turn when God's love feels far away? How do we find strength that overcomes in the midst of doubt?

The God of the Promise

The story of Abraham is one of the most inspiring stories of faith in the Bible. To understand the significance of his story, it's important to step back and remind ourselves of God's bigger story of redemption. The book of Genesis begins with the account of creation, where we learn that God made the heavens and the earth and then created human beings in his image. He gave humanity power and dominion, but rather than using that authority in glad submission to our creator, we sought to establish a life of flourishing without God.

This rebellion introduced sin into the human equation and eventually led to the establishment of a city whose sole purpose was to reach the glory of heaven while avoiding the God who made heaven (Gen. 11). God spoiled the rebellion at the Tower of Babel, and people spread out across the earth as a result. After we learn about this dispersion, the story of Genesis abruptly zooms in and focuses on the life of one old man and his wife. We're introduced to Abraham and Sarah and told that they would play a pivotal role in God's plan to undo the consequences of sin and bring all people back into right relationship with their creator.

God promised to give Abraham a son and that his son would have a family. His family would become a nation and that nation would bring forth a Savior who would rescue the world from sin and reconcile us back to God. The details around how this would all take place were murky at best, but Abraham took God at his word and left his homeland in obedience to God's command.

By the time we get to Genesis 15, Abraham and Sarah had been waiting for their promised son for ten years. They were long past the age of childbearing, and hope deferred had made them heartsick. They were frustrated and discouraged, and so God reaffirmed his promise to bless them. Abraham's response was less than enthusiastic.

"O Sovereign LORD, what good are all your blessings when *I don't even have a son*?" (Gen. 15:2 NLT).

How long could God expect this elderly couple to wait? His repeated promise sounded stale and hollow to Abraham's ears. God might say that a child was coming, but with every passing day, the promise looked more and more ridiculous.

After Abraham responded with discouragement, God called him outside his tent and told him to number the stars. The old man stood there staring into the night sky, and as he did, *something* came alive inside of him. Rather than focusing on his circumstances, his attention shifted onto God himself, who was far greater than any of Abraham's problems and pains. When he took his eyes off himself, faith ignited in his heart (Gen. 15:6).

This was an inspiring moment of faith, but it didn't last long. In fact, just two verses later, we read that Abraham was struggling with his doubts again. "But he said, 'O Lord GOD, how am I to know that I shall possess it?'" (Gen. 15:8 ESV).

Notice how Abraham didn't hide or deny his struggle. He openly processed his doubt with God, inviting God to participate in the fight and walk with him through the questions. Rather than being frustrated with Abraham's unbelief, God led him into one of the most profound spiritual encounters in all of the Bible.

The Covenant of Blessing

"So the LORD said to him, 'Bring me a heifer, a goat and a ram, each three years old, along with a dove and a young pigeon.' Abram brought all these to him, cut them in two and arranged the halves opposite each other" (Gen. 15:9–10).

This is one of those stories in the Bible where everyone in it seemed to understand what was going on, but we as modern readers are left completely in the dark. What were they doing? Why did God ask for these specific animals, and why did Abraham cut them in half?

To understand what was happening, we must consider the cultural gap between Abraham's time and our time. Today, we live in a "written" culture, which means that when an agreement is made, we put it in writing. When you buy a house, it's not officially yours until you sign the papers at the closing. When you get married, it's not official until you sign the marriage certificate. Agreements between two parties are made with pen and paper.

We are so used to this that we erroneously assume that it's the way society has always been. But in Abraham's day, there weren't pens and paper in every house. He lived in an "oral" culture, and in his social structure, audible storytelling *was* the pen, the paper, and the signature.[4] When two parties sought to make a pact, they would act out a story that illustrated the consequences of breaking the promise as a symbol of their commitment.

As soon as Abraham questioned God, God responded in the way that Abraham would understand. He asked for certain animals that represented the traditional covenant-making ceremony of the time. Abraham knew that the first part of the ceremony required that he cut the animals in two, making a path between the pieces. Then a representative of the weaker party would say, "If I fail to keep this promise, may it be done to me as it was done to these animals." After the weaker party had walked between the pieces, a representative of the stronger party would say the same thing. Once both parties had acted out "the curse of the covenant," the deal was done.

This tradition was well-known to the people at the time, and this is why the writer didn't bother to explain how Abraham knew to cut the animals in half. The practice is referenced again in a different context in Jeremiah 34. There we read about an instance when one party did not keep the terms of the agreement. "Because you have broken the terms of our covenant, I will cut you apart just as you cut apart the calf when you walked between its halves to solemnize your vows" (v. 18 NLT). A ceremony like this was taken very seriously, and it was considered binding unto death.

In Genesis 15, God was clearly inviting Abraham into a covenant promise, but as he did this, something strange happened. We read that "as the sun was setting, Abram fell into a deep sleep, and a thick and dreadful darkness came over him.... When the sun had set and darkness had fallen, a smoking firepot with a blazing torch appeared and passed between the pieces. On that day the LORD made a covenant with Abram" (vv. 12, 17–18).

Before Abraham had the chance to walk between the pieces as the representative of the weaker party, he fell asleep. Then God appeared. The language used to describe God's appearance intentionally mirrors the words used in Exodus 19, when he showed up on Mount Sinai in a cloud of smoke and fire. In his encounter with Abraham, God *alone* passed between the pieces, while Abraham simply rested.

This all may seem very strange to us, but to early readers of the story, God's actions would have been culturally unthinkable. It started out fairly normally, with God taking responsibility for his side of the covenant, telling Abraham that he would fulfill his promise of a son and a nation. From this nation, God would bless the world with a Savior.

But the part that would have puzzled early readers was that God never asked Abraham to walk between the pieces. This meant that he was saying to Abraham, "If *you* are unfaithful and do not uphold my covenant, if you doubt, fail, or falter—I, the Lord, will take full responsibility for *your side* of the covenant as well."

At first, this may not seem to make any sense. How could God possibly take responsibility for Abraham's obedience? Why would he agree to suffer in the event of Abraham's failure? God is not a man, like Abraham. Certainly, he couldn't become a man and live a perfect life in the place of Abraham, could he?

As the story of the Bible unfolds, it becomes obvious that the children of Abraham did fail God and did not live up to the covenant promise. They ignored his commands, wandered from his word, and chased other lovers. They doubted and questioned him time and time again. So God did what he promised he would do. He remembered his oath to Abraham and came in the form of a human being. Born of flesh and blood, the offspring of Abraham, he died to bear Abraham's side of the covenant, taking full responsibility for the sins of his people.

When the writer of Hebrews sought to explain the accomplishments of Christ, he wrote, "We have confidence to enter the Most Holy Place by the blood of Jesus, by a new and living way opened for us through the curtain, that is, his body" (10:19–20).

In the temple, a thick curtain marked off the Holy of Holies, where God's tangible presence dwelled. No one could enter this sacred place except for the high priest, and only once per year. Common Israelites could not come this close to God, and the curtain was the barrier that kept them out. The writer of Hebrews informs us that the curtain represented Christ's body.

Just as darkness enveloped Abraham on the day that God made the promise, so darkness surrounded Christ as he hung on the cross. "Darkness came over the whole land until three in the afternoon, for the sun stopped shining. And *the curtain of the temple was torn in two.* Jesus called out with a loud voice, 'Father, into your hands I commit my spirit.' When he had said this, he breathed his last" (Luke 23:44–46).

According to Luke's account, the last thing that happened as Jesus died on the cross was the curtain in the temple was mysteriously torn in two. As if God himself reached down and ripped it in half, the separation between God and his people came down. But why would Luke mention this curtain? Because the covenant ceremony between God and Abraham had to be fulfilled. On the cross, Jesus Christ was torn in two, so to speak. His body *was* the curtain. He became just like those animals.

Jesus was torn apart by sin so that God's promise to bless and favor Abraham would be transferred from Abraham to Jesus, to *you*. "And now that you belong to Christ, you are the true children of Abraham. You are his heirs, and God's promise to Abraham belongs to you" (Gal. 3:29 NLT).

God connected the dots of history and sent Jesus to uphold Abraham's side of the covenant so he could pour out his blessing on those who don't deserve it. Abraham "believed the LORD, and he credited it to him as righteousness" (Gen. 15:6). This is the essence of the gospel—right standing with God that comes by grace through faith.

Grace requires an internal shift, where the recipient relies fully on God's favor rather than his own performance. It requires that we consciously choose to look away from ourselves—our worthiness, strength, and ability—and instead look only to God. This is how we find the greater, unshakable assurance and learn to overcome the doubt that would seek to rule our hearts.

The Great Yes

When the apostle Paul sought to explain the blessings available to us in Christ, he told the Christians in Corinth, "The Son of God, Jesus Christ, whom we proclaimed among you ... was not Yes and No, but in him it is *always Yes*. For all the promises of God find their Yes in him. That is why it is through him that we utter our Amen to God for his glory" (2 Cor. 1:19–20 ESV).

Jesus lived the life that you could not, and he died the death that you deserve. As the offspring of Abraham, he perfectly fulfilled humanity's side of the covenant that God made with Abraham in Genesis 15. Thousands of promises fill the pages of Scripture—promises of eternal life, peace, victory, and power. In our own righteousness, we do not deserve any of these promises, and that's why Jesus stepped in.

For him, every promise of God is *yes*. Because of his perfect standing before the Father, he deserves a "yes" every time, but the gospel goes a step further, teaching us that the "yes" of Jesus now belongs to *you*. You can't earn it and you don't deserve it, but if you will utter an "amen," which means "I agree," then these promises become yours. To experience the reality of the blessing, you must take him at his word.

In Romans 8, Paul further explained the rationale of God in promising to bless you. "He who did not spare his own Son, but gave him up for us all—how will he not also, along with him, graciously give us *all* things?" (v. 32).

To fully understand Romans 8:32, which some scholars have called the most important verse in the Bible, we must grasp the logic behind the argument. Paul was using what in Latin is called an *a for-tiori* argument.[5] This means he was calculating the impact of Christ's sacrifice through a rational comparison.

An *a fortiori* argument (literally, "from a stronger") compares the greater to the lesser.[6] For example, if Joe the bodybuilder can lift five hundred pounds over his head, then it's obvious that Joe can also lift a ten-pound weight over his head. This is an argument from the greater to the lesser. It means that the ten-pound weight is included in Joe's strength capacity, because he has already done far more.

The Bible teaches that the bond between God the Father and God the Son is the strongest, deepest bond in the universe. The Father and Son have forever remained in an eternal bond of love, and of all the expressions of love that have ever been or will ever be, nothing comes close to this.

But something happened on Calvary that reshaped the world forever. God did not spare his own Son but gave him up for us all. The Father handed the Son over to be crucified for the sins of the world, and this was the heaviest lift in history.

Nothing harder or more sacrificial has ever been done. Therefore, since God has already done the hardest and most loving and gracious thing imaginable, how will he not also, along with him, graciously give us *all things*? Every promise is yes. All things are yours.

Made Complete

Where will you turn when God's love feels far away? How will you find strength in the moments of doubt? Turn to his Word. Every promise belongs to you. Memorize it. Study it. Submit to it. Rehearse it. Allow his truth to speak a better word over your feelings and thoughts, and as you declare his Word over your life, your inner and outer world will begin to come into alignment with him.

For years I've kept a folder with key verses and phrases from the Bible. Every morning in my time of prayer, I open the folder and pull out those weathered pieces of paper where I've written the promises of God. I read them out loud, day after day, and without fail as I do, I can sense something changing inside of me. The Spirit of God goes to work as I take him at his word.

I don't always understand what God is doing. In fact, most of the time I can't see what will happen next. His ways are far higher than our ways. But in the midst of an uncertain world, his Word is a lamp and a light. If you will meditate on it and center your life on it, his living Word will make you whole. Consider the implications of his Word in your life.

"All Scripture is breathed out by God and profitable for *teaching*, for *reproof*, for *correction*, and for *training* in righteousness, that the man of God may be *complete*, equipped for every good work" (2 Tim. 3:16–17 ESV).

First, Scripture is our great teacher. Learn to be a student of his Word and allow it to reshape the way you think. Second, the word *reproof* means "to expose." It's like how a detective reviews the evidence and exposes the truth. God's Word functions like a detective in our hearts, showing us things we can't otherwise see and explaining things we can't otherwise understand. Third, his Word corrects. In this context, *correction* means "to repair something that's broken." God's Word is like a general contractor, overseeing a massive renovation on the inside.

Last, Scripture serves as a trainer. A good coach knows what you are capable of even more than you know it yourself. In the same way,

God's Word will push you beyond your limits so that you can discover the life that he's intended for you. All these functions of the Word of God in your life lead to one thing: *wholeness*. You are made complete (i.e., brought to completeness).

There's something else in this verse that's worth noting. Paul used a very specific phrase to describe the person who takes God at his word. He wrote "that *the man of God* may be complete." In the original Greek language, this term "man of God" is *Theos anthropos*. For any Jew familiar with the Greek translation of the Old Testament, this was a special title in the Bible. It appears over sixty times in Scripture, and it's always reserved for God's most anointed leaders.

Moses, Samuel, Elijah—these men were all referred to by the term *Theos anthropos*. They were the ones who called down fire from heaven, parted the seas, and led a nation. But here in 2 Timothy, Paul reached back in history and applied this ancient title to all of those who would take God at his word. Because of Jesus, the power of the *Theos anthropos* is available to *you*. You are now "the Man of God" or "the Woman of God."

What would happen if you allowed his Word to have first place in your life? What would happen if you aggressively applied it to your biggest doubts and largest problems? Charles Spurgeon had this to say about the power of the Word:

> There seems to me to have been twice as much done
> in some ages in defending the Bible as in expounding
> it, but if the whole of our strength shall henceforth
> go to the exposition and spreading of it, we may
> leave it pretty much to defend itself. I do not know

whether you see that lion—it is very distinctly before my eyes; a number of persons advance to attack him, while a host of us would defend him.... Pardon me if I offer a quiet suggestion. Open the door and let the lion out; he will take care of himself. Why, they are gone! He no sooner goes forth in his strength than his assailants flee. The way to meet infidelity is to spread the Bible. The answer to every objection against the Bible is the Bible.[7]

Let the lion out. Take God at his word. Then watch as the hurricane quiets down and the sea becomes still.

CHAPTER 5

OUR PROVIDER
Learning to see God as your source

> *"And Abraham lifted up his eyes and*
> *looked, and behold, behind him was a*
> *ram, caught in a thicket by his horns."*
> Genesis 22:13 (ESV)

It took the fire department more than forty-five minutes to respond. As we waited, we watched our twenty-eight-foot RV burn down to the tires.

My friends and I had formed a music group. We were just wrapping up an eleven-day tour through the Adirondacks when the engine began to smoke. When we pulled over on Route 73 East in New York, we discovered that the engine was on fire. We quickly got all nine people off the RV, and then we watched helplessly as our clothes, computers, phones, and instruments went up in flames. My wife and one-year-old son stood at my side. As cars stopped and tried to help, we realized that no one had cell phone reception and there was nothing we could do but wait.

I remember the feeling when we finally got back to our friend's house a few hours later, still stinking like smoke and relieved to be alive. We had lost everything, and as a bunch of young adults in our early twenties, we had no plan B. I closed the door to my friend's guest room and got on my knees to pray. It didn't take long before I ran out of words. Then, in the quiet, I heard a faint inner voice. *This is your promotion.*

The thought made me laugh out loud. I had purchased the most basic vehicle insurance available, and I knew that none of what we lost would be covered. I was grateful that no one had been seriously injured in the fire, but I couldn't see how this could possibly serve as a promotion.

In a moment of inspiration, we gathered everyone together who had been in the RV, and we all wrote down every single item we had lost. The lists were long. There were sneakers, headphones, cell phones, and watches, and it added up to tens of thousands of dollars. We put our lists into one pile, put our hands on the lists, and prayed a simple prayer. "God, help."

To our surprise, he did. Over the next few weeks, God used hundreds of people and a host of inexplicable coincidences to enable us to replace everything we had lost. We saw miracle after miracle, and we ended up with newer, better equipment. In a strange way, we *had* been promoted, and as a twenty-four-year-old kid trying to grow in my relationship with God, the experience changed me.

The fire began a deep and fundamental shift in my perspective that continues to evolve and expand today. In some ways, the change on the inside has been hard to quantify, but this experience revealed to my heart something fundamental about God. He is a present "help in times of trouble" (Ps. 46:1 NLT). He wants us to call to him in our distress (Jer. 33:3). God doesn't want to be our third or fourth option—he wants to train us to turn to him *first* and see him as our source.

In the Pixar movie *Finding Nemo*, Marlin is the overly protective, constantly worried father (and clown fish). Early in the movie, we learn that Marlin's wife and other kids were attacked and eaten by a larger fish, leaving only him and his son, Nemo, as survivors. This loss leads Marlin to develop a compulsion for control and an obsessive tendency to know where his son is at all times. When Nemo ends up getting lost, Marlin loses his mind.

There's a classic scene in the movie when Marlin fearfully says to his friend Dori, "I promised that I would never let anything happen to him."

Dori responds, "Hmm. That's a funny thing to promise. You can't never let anything happen to him. Then nothing would ever happen to him."

Her words carry a profound insight. When things get out of control in life, our natural impulse is to squeeze. We try to keep every circumstance in our grasp, but no matter how tightly we hold on, life will never fully submit to our will. It's unpredictable and often inexplicable. To try to control everything ruins the good things in life. As unnerving as it seems, we must all come to terms with the fact that *we are not in control*.

Maybe you got yourself through college or started a business. You climbed your way up the corporate ladder and the experience taught you that with enough hard work and determination, you *can* control your life. After a little while you've got some money in the bank, and you start to feel like you can actually handle anything.

> To try to control everything ruins the good things in life. As unnerving as it seems, we must all come to terms with the fact that *we are not in control.*

Most of us love this feeling and cling to it tightly, but inevitably, something will happen that pushes us beyond what we can control. When tragedy hits or problems arise that we can't fix, our lack of control often comes as a shock to many of us. We scramble and struggle—or like Marlin, we completely fall apart.

What will you do when no matter how hard you try, you can't fix it, change it, heal it, or help it? What will you do when life forces you to face the end of your own strength? There are really only three options: you can try to maintain the mirage and deny reality, you can just fall apart and spiral into despair, or you can look beyond yourself and allow God to radically reshape your perspective.

Reshaping Perspective

Throughout the Bible, God made constant references to the human senses, frequently telling those he interacted with to open their eyes and listen with their ears (2 Kings 6:17; Matt. 11:15). His commands are intended to reveal our need to develop an "inner awareness" that goes beyond the natural senses. Paul called this awareness "learning to see with the eyes of your heart" (see Eph. 1:18).

One person sees a sunrise, while another person looks at the same scene and sees the artwork of heaven. The Pharisees saw uneducated fishermen and tax collectors, but Jesus saw apostles and world changers.

The work of God in our lives often boils down to the reshaping of our perspective. Two people can be presented with the same evidence and interpret it in completely different ways. Maybe you've seen this picture of the old woman.

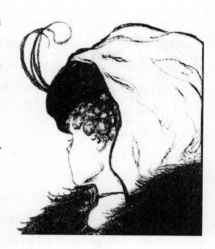

Notice her massive nose, sunken eyes, and long chin. She appears to have no neck at all as her fur coat is wrapped around her shoulders. But from another perspective, a young woman appears. She wears a necklace on her long neck, and her face is turned away from the viewer. What was once the nose of the older woman now appears to be the jawline of the young woman. After a bit of effort, are you able to see both?

Too often in life, we see things from only one point of view, and this leads to false conclusions about God. For example, Christians love to repeat the phrase "God is good, all the time," but the meaning of that phrase is often lost on us. What does it really mean to say that God is good all the time? Without realizing it, many professing Christians have come to believe that the phrase means "God keeps me comfortable all the time." We say it after we get a promotion at work or find a parking spot close to the entrance of the store.

But do we say it when someone in our family gets sick? Do we say it when we are passed up for the promotion? God doesn't seem very good in those moments.

We love to pray for a "hedge of protection" and, like Marlin, hope that nothing will ever happen to us. We hope to avoid problems, skip hardships, and navigate around trials, but when this expectation isn't met, our faith wabbles. Is God still good then?

The problem is rooted in our perspective. We tend to see God one-dimensionally, when sometimes a single picture reveals the images of two women rather than just one. God is actually still good in the blessings and in the trials, but until we learn this truth for ourselves, we will constantly misinterpret the challenges we face. How could the burning down of an RV be a promotion? God was inviting us into a promotion in perspective, and he does that by introducing a *test*.

The New Testament author James wrote,

> Dear brothers and sisters, when troubles of any kind come your way, consider it an opportunity for great joy. For you know that when your faith is *tested*, your endurance has a chance to grow. So let it grow, for when your endurance is fully developed, you will be perfect and complete, needing nothing. (James 1:2–4 NLT)

In this text, James outlined a radically counterintuitive perspective. Our comfort-driven culture has taught us to see trials as exclusively bad things, but according to James, God uses trials for something good. So good, in fact, that as we learn to see with the eyes of our heart, trials themselves are transformed into opportunities for "great joy."

Throughout the pages of Scripture, we find examples of how God uses trials to grow his people. We are told in the Psalms, "For you, God, *tested us*; you refined us like silver" (66:10), and in Proverbs, "The crucible for silver and the furnace for gold, but the LORD *tests the heart*" (17:3). Just as fine metals require fire if they are to be purified and made beautiful, so God uses trials to make beautiful the human heart. God tests Christians, and you can be sure that he is testing you right now.

Does something inside of you wince when you think about this? Does the idea of life as a test contradict your understanding of God? If so, this is evidence that you haven't yet seen the full picture. Moses told the people of Israel in the wilderness, "Do not be afraid. God has come to *test you*" (Ex. 20:20).

Most of us have learned through experience to view tests with a level of trepidation. No one likes going for their driver's test, and no one looks forward to their algebra final. We've internalized the idea that tests are bad, and we struggle to see how a good God could let his children be tested. But what we must realize is that without the challenge of the driver's test, we wouldn't have the freedom of the driver's license. Without the difficulty of the algebra final, we wouldn't have the opportunity that comes with the diploma. Testing prepares us for greater freedom, and this is what God is up to in every test. He uses the test to set you free.

In his extensive research on the topic of resilience, statistician Nassim Taleb made a distinction between the fragile, the robust, and the antifragile.[1] Fragile things avoid variations and strain because they can't handle the shock that a test causes to the system. Imagine a glass cup that's thrown against a brick wall. There's a very high probability that it will break because the cup is fragile.

We often assume that the opposite of being fragile is to be robust. Robust things can take the shock and remain unchanged. Think of a plastic mug that bounces off the brick wall instead of shattering. The mug absorbs the shock and is not damaged by it. But according to Taleb, there is a third category, which he called "antifragile."

Antifragile things actually benefit from the variations, shocks, randomness, and strain. They carry a unique quality that enables them to get stronger when tested. Taleb wrote that "wind extinguishes a candle and energizes fire."[2] The candle is fragile and goes out when the wind blows, but the fire absorbs the wind and becomes stronger because of it.

Nature teaches us that the human body frequently functions in antifragile ways. Lifting weights, for example, tears the muscles and strains the nervous system, but it results in stronger bones and bigger muscles. When a vaccine is introduced into the body, the small dose of the disease strengthens the immune system, enabling us to fight off the illness in the future.

Taleb continued, "It is said that the best horses lose when they compete with slower ones, and win against better rivals. Under-compensation from the absence of a stressor ... absence of challenge, degrades the best of the best."[3]

God understands us far better than we understand ourselves, and in his sovereign plan to reveal his glory in the world, he has chosen to permit trials and tests and use them to reshape our perspective and refine our character. The artist Michelangelo said of his famous statue of David, "I saw the angel in the marble, and I carved until I set it free." This is a fitting example of the work of God in our hearts. He can see in us what we can't yet see in ourselves, and sometimes this means that something significant must be chipped away.

Just because God uses trials and allows for tests, it doesn't mean that he causes all the bad things that happen in this life. God is *good*, and the evil in the world comes from demons, sin, and a broken humanity. But God is also above it all, working all things together to unveil his majesty and bless his children (Rom. 8:28). Sometimes God shows us his goodness by blessing us, and other times God shows us his goodness by growing us through a test.

Every test is an invitation to a new perspective. If we let it, the test can reshape our values, restructure our self-image, and strengthen our convictions. In nearly every culture and people group on earth, initiation ceremonies and rites of passage have played a critical part in moving people into maturity. Young men must be tested if they are to step into manhood, and young women must be tested if they are to mature into womanhood. Whether you realize it or not, you *need* the test, and your faith can't become antifragile until it faces a few storms.

The Great Test

In the previous chapter, we explored the story in Genesis 15 where God made a covenant promise to Abraham. God's promise of a son eventually did come to pass, and Isaac was born. It's hard to imagine what Abraham and Sarah must have felt about their boy after decades of hoping and praying for a son. Isaac was the apple of their eye, the living embodiment of the goodness of God toward them.

How shocking and painful it must have been, then, when after years of joyfully celebrating God's kindness and faithfulness, Abraham heard God speak again:

> Some time later God tested Abraham. He said to him, "Abraham!"
>
> "Here I am," he replied.
>
> Then God said, "Take your son, your only son, whom you love—Isaac—and go to the region of Moriah. Sacrifice him there as a burnt offering on a mountain I will show you." (Gen. 22:1–2)

Notice how the author began by telling us that this was a test for Abraham. God's intentions were not vindictive or unkind. He tested Abraham because he loved him. But even so, these words must have felt like an atomic bomb in Abraham's heart.

Sacrifice Isaac? There must be some mistake. God isn't like the pagan deities of Canaan. How could he ask Abraham to do this? Abraham knew that it was God who had given him and Sarah the promise of a miracle son in the first place, and it was God who had miraculously provided the child. Abraham must have felt that this command was in direct contradiction to everything he knew about the character of God, and that's why it was a test.

Just like Abraham, you and I will face moments when it seems as if the commands of God just don't add up. All you can see is the face of the old woman. All you can see is the sickness or the sadness or the loss. How could God still be good? The second face remains hidden from your eyes. For every person who chooses to trust God, the day of contradiction will most certainly come, and the test will show whether it's God or your own reason that holds first place in your life.

Did Abraham love Isaac more than he loved God? An invisible competition seemed to be going on in his heart since God called Isaac "your son, your *only* son, whom you *love*." Maybe Abraham had allowed the gift to become more important than the giver. Maybe Abraham had gotten comfortable and had disconnected from the life of frontier faith.

When God tests our hearts, he often does it by commanding us to give up something we love. God himself doesn't need anything, but he calls us to make sacrifices in order to train our hearts to rely on him as our source. Although this may feel like an unloving demand, it is actually a deeply loving act on God's part. He knows that *he* is what we need most. He alone can provide us with ultimate peace, joy, and satisfaction. Therefore, calling us to sacrifice trains our hearts in this truth.

Some people wrongly assume that since God is God, he can do anything, but there are certain things that even God cannot do. For example, God cannot lie, since he is the perfect truth, and he cannot learn, since he already knows all things. In the same way, God cannot "be second." He can only be first. This is called the preeminence of God, and when we treat him as second in our lives, we find ourselves out of step with reality.

> **When God tests our hearts, he often does it by commanding us to give up something we love. Although this may feel like an unloving demand, it is actually a deeply loving act on God's part. He knows that *he* is what we need most.**

The preeminence of God, which we might also call the "principle of the first," teaches that if we will actively put God first in all things, he will prove to be our unending source. From this inner posture of the heart, we will experience his favor and power. Since we are naturally inclined toward selfishness, putting God first requires a radical step of faith.

In the book of Genesis, Cain and Abel each brought an offering to the Lord. God rejected Cain's offering but accepted Abel's. It might have been that Abel brought the first and the best of his herds, and Cain brought the extras or leftovers of his crops (4:3–5). If so, then Abel acknowledged the preeminence of God and gave of his "first," while Cain gave only what was left.

When we give to God first, it constitutes an act of faith, since there is no guarantee that we will have enough. But when we give God only what's left over, we've already made sure that we are provided for. One way trains our hearts to trust God, while the other trains our hearts to maintain control.

In the book of Exodus, God instructed Moses that the firstborn of all of Israel's animals belonged to the Lord (13:2). Why would he do this? Again, it was a test. He was teaching the Israelites the principle of the first. If the firstborn animal had to be sacrificed to God, then every time an Israelite made such a sacrifice, they had to wrestle with their own sense of control. What if their livestock never had a second offspring? What if they made the sacrifice and then they were left with nothing?

There's an intriguing story in 1 Kings 17 that profoundly illustrates the principle of the first. A famine had swept across the land, and God promised to provide for the prophet Elijah through the generosity of a widow in a foreign city. Elijah traveled to the city and found the widow, but it seemed that God never told her that she'd be making food for the prophet.

When Elijah arrived, the widow was gathering sticks at the gate of the city (1 Kings 17:10). This small detail is intended to tell us a few things about the widow. First, she was so poor that she didn't even have money for firewood. Widows at that time often suffered from extreme economic hardship, since women did not hold the same authority as men, and they had no social system to help meet the needs of the family if the husband died.

The Hebrew phrase used to describe the gathering of sticks appears only a few other times in the Bible. The first time is when the people of Israel were enslaved in Egypt and Pharaoh forced them to gather straw to make bricks. His expectations were unrealistic, and the oppression of Pharaoh caused the people to cry out in despair. Their frantic "gathering" was a symbol of their slavery.

The second time the phrase is used is in Numbers 15, when a man ignored the Sabbath command to rest and instead gathered sticks to make a fire. He was unwilling to trust God as his source, and he set aside the law of God to provide for himself. In both instances, gathering sticks is a physical symbol of the inner tendency toward self-salvation. Rather than turning to God, *you* will solve your problems. You will carry the weight of your life because you think that the strength you need can come from *in* you.

As Elijah approached this widow at the gate, the author used this physical activity of stick gathering to give the reader a clue into her inner condition. She did not see God as her provider. She was clinging and clawing for life, trying desperately to survive on her own strength.

Her experience of lack had produced in her a scarcity mentality. She lived under constant pressure. She expected the worst around every corner. She wrestled with the fear of not having enough. This was a picture of a person who did not live with God as her source.

When Elijah asked the widow for bread, she responded by telling him, "I don't have any bread—only a handful of flour in a jar and a little olive oil in a jug. I am gathering a few sticks to take home and make a meal for myself and my son, that we may eat it—and die" (1 Kings 17:12). Her scarcity mentality had brought her to the edge of despair, and Elijah's response served as the turning point in the story:

> Elijah said to her, "Don't be afraid. Go home and do as you have said. But *first* make a small loaf of bread for me from what you have and bring it to me, and then make something for yourself and your son. For this is what the LORD, the God of Israel, says: 'The jar of flour will not be used up and the jug of oil will not run dry until the day the LORD sends rain on the land.'" (1 Kings 17:13–14)

Elijah instructed the woman to take the tiny bit of food that she had and make something for him *first*. To the modern reader, this sounds cruel and selfish on Elijah's part, but Elijah understood the principle of the first. He knew that through her radical act of faith, God would step in—and that was exactly what happened. The widow chose to trust God, and God multiplied her resources and met her need (1 Kings 17:16).

Likewise, when God instructed Abraham to climb up the mountain and sacrifice his son, he was testing Abraham's faith and claiming first place in his heart. Surprisingly, Abraham didn't ask any questions. He didn't hesitate. He just cut the wood, loaded the donkey, and set out with Isaac to the place where God told him to go. But how could he be so robotic? Where were his tears and his pleading with God? We don't find anything like that.

The author portrays Abraham this way so the reader will catch a glimpse of the bigger storyline. At this point in the story, Abraham was not the same man that he was in Genesis 15, when he doubted God and had to go gaze at the stars in the night sky. What was once "theory" for Abraham had now become a deep, unwavering conviction.

Abraham spent the better part of his life learning to trust God, and he made plenty of mistakes along the way. He had been tested through wars, tested through suffering, tested with Ishmael, and tested through long stretches of waiting. The precious metals of his heart had been refined again and again, and they now had reached a state of profound clarity. Abraham wasn't perfect, but he was convinced of one thing: God *is good*, all the time. And if God wanted him to sacrifice Isaac, he believed that somehow, even through this, God had something good in store.

The Bible gives us a window into Abraham's thinking when he told his servants to wait at the bottom of the mountain: "Stay here with the donkey while I and the boy go over there. We will worship and then *we* will come back to you" (Gen. 22:5).

If he was going to sacrifice his son, why would he say that they both would return? The writer of the book of Hebrews noticed this clue and concluded that "Abraham reasoned that God could even raise the dead, and so in a manner of speaking he did receive Isaac back from death" (11:19).

This is incredible, since at this point in the biblical storyline, no one had ever been raised from the dead. But Abraham saw into the heart of God. He caught a glimpse into the multidimensional nature of God's plans, and he concluded that God was so good that there was no way that Isaac would be lost. God had promised to build a nation through Isaac and bring forth a Savior, and those promises had not yet been fulfilled. This left only one other option: God would raise the dead.

Abraham understood that sometimes God does take things away from us, but he also had come to believe that God, at his core, is *not* a taker. The very nature of God is to give. He is a giver, and anything good that God takes away, he always intends to resurrect. All of this led Abraham to conclude that he could fully entrust Isaac's life to God, knowing that God would eventually reveal his good plan.

The God Who Provides

Just as Abraham raised the knife to take the life of his son, God intervened and told him to stop. Abraham had passed the test. At that very moment, he looked up and saw a ram caught in the nearby thicket. He then sacrificed the ram in place of his son. "So Abraham called that place The LORD Will Provide" (Gen. 22:14).

The English word *provide* comes from the Latin *pro*, meaning "on behalf of," and *vide*, meaning "to see." It describes someone who recognizes a need and makes sure that the need is met. They see it through. They "see to it." It's the same root word that's found in the term *providence*. The providence of God describes God's commitment to see all of his creation and work his good plan through all things.

Abraham named this place The LORD Will Provide so that for all time future generations could learn this truth about God. He is the provider. He is the source. He sees you and he's committed to seeing you through. To live your life trying to provide for yourself is like the widow gathering sticks. It leads only to slavery, worry, and unending grasping, and it never leads to peace.

One intriguing detail in this story is that Abraham didn't see the ram until he had lifted the knife to sacrifice his son. A ram is a full-grown male sheep. Smaller rams weigh about 120 pounds, while larger rams can weigh over 500 pounds. This is not a small animal, and it would not have been quiet if it were stuck in a nearby bush.

Have you ever seen an animal trapped in a thornbush, struggling to get out? I recently saw a video of a horse stuck in mud. It thrashed and neighed and flailed its body all over the place. It makes no sense that Abraham wouldn't have been aware of this animal while he was tying Isaac to the altar. But he didn't see or hear the ram because *God's provision isn't fully seen until we are tested, and we surrender.*

This is why so few Christians really experience God as their source. We tend to hedge and to bargain. We trust God with half our hearts while we cling to our false notions of control. We often look more like Marlin than Abraham. We might experience glimpses of God's provision, but we don't see radical miracles because the ram only becomes visible once we've surrendered what we love most.

Remember the *Back to the Future* movies? In the third movie, Doc and Marty need to get the time machine up to eighty-eight miles per hour before they reach the edge of a cliff and run out of track. They mark a point in the track with a sign that reads "The Point of No Return." They know that once they reach that place, they can't slow down fast enough to save their lives or their time machine. They're either launching through time or launching off the cliff. There is no turning back.

This is exactly where God leads us through the tests of life. He brings us along, proving his faithfulness every step of the way, until we reach the place of no turning back.

And that's why this story is so important, because the confidence we need to trust God as our provider is found in the details. God worked through the actual events of Abraham's life to foreshadow the greatest event in history. This future event would serve as iron-clad evidence for all time that God can be trusted and that he is the provider.

Just as Isaac was Abraham's only son—the son of his love—so Jesus is God's one and only Son. Jesus carried the wood up the mountain just as Isaac did, but when God lifted his knife to slay his only Son, there was no intervention. God did what Abraham was spared from doing. He gave his first and best, experienced the deepest anguish, and revealed through the sacrifice his very heart. God is not a taker. At his core, at his very depths, he is a giver.

As the ram was the substitute for Isaac, so Christ was the substitute for us. Through this story, God prepares us to understand true substitutionary atonement. Someone would stand in our place. Someone had to absorb our debt. Christ was the one who had the thorns wrapped around his head just as the ram was caught in the thorny thicket.

In the book of Genesis, thorns and thistles are introduced as symbols of the curse (3:18–19). We saw how the connection to the curse was displayed through the snake, and God gives us another picture to illustrate the same idea through the thorns. Jesus wore the curse as a crown so that we could wear his crown of life (James 1:12).

After the experience with the ram, Abraham said, "On the mountain of the LORD it *will be* provided" (Gen. 22:14). He was prophesying as he stood on Mount Moriah, the place where the Jerusalem temple would be built generations later. This would also be the place where Jesus would be tried, convicted, and condemned to die.

On the mountain of the Lord, it was provided. Your sins were forgiven through his sacrifice. God "saw it through," and when we see with the eyes of the heart, we find the confidence we need to trust his goodness completely. Jesus is our proof that God is a giver. He has not come to rob you. He has come to bless you, and when you believe this, you can trust him with everything.

Living from the Source

The Philippian church of the first century was one of the most radically generous communities in history. Their generosity was famous among the churches of the New Testament (2 Cor. 8:2), and in his letter to the church of Philippi, the apostle Paul thanked them for their sacrificial lifestyle. But before he concluded the letter, Paul made sure that these Christians knew the heart of God toward them. He wrote, "And my God will supply *every need of yours* according to his riches in glory in Christ Jesus" (Phil. 4:19 ESV).

Every need supplied—this is an amazing promise. Paul didn't qualify his statement or put limits around it, and that makes most of us uncomfortable. But the more we learn to trust God as our endless supply, the more we see with the eyes of the heart. This life is not all there is, and his promise extends far beyond our time on earth. He will not forget his promise, and eternity will prove that he never fails to provide for those who trust him.

Paul affirmed this truth when he wrote to the Corinthian church, "Remember this: Whoever sows sparingly will also reap sparingly, and whoever sows generously will also reap generously.... And God is able to bless you abundantly, so that in all things at all times, having all that you need, you will abound in every good work" (2 Cor. 9:6, 8).

As we learn to cling to these promises, they cause a deep shift in our hearts, and the result is an inexplicable peace. No more gathering sticks. No more flailing or grasping for control.

Understanding God as your source changes everything about life. We no longer serve him out of a nervous attempt to earn his favor, since we know that we already have his favor through Jesus. We don't strain to prove our own worthiness through our efforts, but instead, we learn to serve God from the strength he supplies.

Peter described this inner shift when he wrote, "If anyone serves, they should do so with the strength God provides" (1 Pet. 4:11). As we turn again and again to the truth of his great love for us in Christ, our service to God flows from that love. The result is not less commitment but more, and that's why Paul could say, "I worked harder than all of them—yet not I, but the *grace* of God that was with me" (1 Cor. 15:10).

These truths lead us into a life of generosity and sacrifice, and they also lead us into joy, because we have a father who always provides for his children. As we experience his supernatural provision, we learn to put down our pile of sticks and continually warm ourselves at the fire of his love.

CHAPTER 6

THE NEW SAFETY
Redefining security on God's terms

"So make yourself an ark of cypress wood; make rooms in it and coat it with pitch inside and out."

Genesis 6:14

It is one of the most beautiful places I have ever seen. West of the Dead Sea, the desert oasis of Ein Gedi has become a popular spot for hiking and exploring for thousands of visitors every year. The landscape is stunning. Towering cliffs and seemingly endless caves surround breathtaking waterfalls and winding streams. The caves meander throughout the mountainous region, and hikers have been marking their routes for thousands of years.

Tradition teaches that the oasis of Ein Gedi was one of David's favorite retreats. It's where he hid from Saul during his years in the desert and where he wrote many of his famous psalms. Walking those paths between the cliffs made the poems of David feel fresh and alive again. I could see what he meant when he wrote, "He leads me beside still waters. He restores my soul" (Ps. 23:2–3 ESV). Ein Gedi felt like the perfect place to rest.

Until a little fly landed on my elbow.

I didn't think much of the fly at first. It looked like any other fly, and I barely felt it bite me. But about an hour later, after we had left the desert oasis, I looked down at my elbow and realized that it was beginning to swell. My skin was turning red and then purple. I mentioned it to our tour guide, and his face went pale. "We need to go to the hospital," he said.

"The hospital? For what?"

Within minutes, we had left the tour behind and were on our way to the emergency room. What I learned on the way was that certain flies in that desert region of the country can kill you with just one bite. Although they are rare, the swelling on my arm was of significant concern. With these deadly flies, first your skin swells, and then it turns purple. Within a few hours you start to have trouble breathing.

As I learned more about the possible implications of my fly bite, I could feel my body responding. My euphoric reflections on the psalms were long gone, and the distinct feeling of panic began spreading. I tried to stay calm, but there was no denying the sense of anxiety that was creeping over me.

We got to the hospital and, after some waiting, met the doctor on call, who didn't speak any English. Our tour guide translated as best he could, and I was soon given some medicine and sent on my way. The medical team at the ER told me they really had no way of knowing what type of fly had bitten me, and the best thing to do was to wait and see. They said that if I started to have trouble breathing, I should come back to the hospital.

Wait and see? At this point, I was definitely having some trouble breathing, but I don't think it had anything to do with the fly bite. Fear had found its way into my heart. As the day went on, not much changed. I didn't start choking or pass out, and eventually the swelling went down. Soon, my arm returned to normal, but the subtle feelings of fear lingered for days. Even as I write this, I can feel them again.

Researchers have found that fear makes a deep mark on our souls. We remember sounds, odors, and small details from moments of increased panic or tension. Oftentimes without our realizing it, these memories become triggers that pull us back into a state of anxiety.[1] We've all experienced this. Maybe you were in a car accident and now every time you get on that same highway, the memory comes flooding back. Or maybe you lost a loved one and you can still remember the dinner that you ate after the funeral. Fear burrows its way into our memories like a determined squirrel in a tree, and it stakes its claim in our hearts.

A few weeks ago, I walked into a YMCA for the first time in twenty years. As soon as I smelled the chlorine from the pool, I felt a tinge of anxiety. The smell transports me back to the swimming lessons I had as a little kid, and for whatever reason, those lessons were terrifying for me at the time. Even now, I can't seem to stop my body from reminding me all these years later.

God knows all about our inner propensity to fear. That's why the most frequently repeated command in the Bible is "fear not." It's stated hundreds of times in dozens of different instances, but hearing the command and obeying the command are two very different things. How do we learn to "fear not," and is that even a realistic expectation in our modern world?

Of all the human emotions, fear is particularly complex. It has layers and levels to it, and this is what makes it so difficult to overcome. There are healthy fears, like the fear of a hot stove or of falling off a roof. These types of fears are essential to life, and they are hardwired into our psyche for our own protection. But every healthy fear can quickly become exaggerated and irrational. The fear of a hot stove can evolve into an unreasonable concern that your house is going to burn down at any moment. The fear of falling off a roof can quickly become a phobia of heights that stops you from taking three steps up a ladder.

Our healthy fears are always just one degree away from becoming unhealthy fears, and every rational concern can quickly spiral into an irrational one. Some people fear spiders, while others fear snakes. Some people fear confrontation, while others fear solitude. Add to these common fears the traumas, losses, and sorrows of life, and we are all surrounded by fear-conditioned cues that trigger feelings of danger.[2]

The English poet John Keats wrote, "There is nothing stable in the world; uproar's your only music,"[3] and it seems that we all know the tune. How do we live at peace in the midst of the incessant soundtrack of uproar? How do we find inner stability in a world of constant instability? For most people, the answer to these questions is the relentless pursuit of *safety*.

Feeling Safe

Safety has taken center stage in our modern culture. It drives our spending, shapes our convictions, and redirects our behavior on an almost daily basis, and its grip on society has multiplied in a very short time. For example, as a kid growing up, I never wore a helmet when I rode my bike. I was a child of the 1990s, and helmet-wearing among the younger generation was only just getting traction at the time. Of all the kids in our neighborhood, only one even had a bike helmet, and we mercilessly made fun of him for it. I can still remember all the times my friend Casey would hide his bike helmet in the woods because he didn't want to be the only kid wearing one.

Fast-forward just a few decades later, and nearly everyone is wearing a helmet. It's become a social taboo *not* to wear one, and parents who let their kids ride helmet-less are looked down on. It's unthinkable. It's borderline unethical. I admit that my kids wear helmets, and I'm not suggesting that wearing one is a bad idea, but it is one small example of our growing cultural focus on safety.

Do you have security cameras installed around your house or an alarm system on your doors? More people than ever answer yes to those questions. Do you carry life insurance, health insurance, car insurance, and homeowner's insurance? All of these things have their place, but the driving goal behind them is the same: more safety.

This focus toward safety coincides with the cultural shift away from faith. As our society relies less and less on God, we've come to see safety as our exclusive responsibility. God isn't going to protect us, so we must keep ourselves safe. The world is unstable and unpredictable, and it's now up to us to create our own bubble of protection.

Unexpectedly, our helmet-wearing, insurance-buying, camera-installing generation isn't becoming less anxious and more secure. The more we seek safety through natural means alone, the more our fears seem to expand. The insurance isn't enough. The cameras aren't enough. Soon we don't just need helmets; we need elbow pads and kneepads too. We find ourselves tracking our loved ones on their phones every time they're out of the house. We freak out and yell at our kids if they unbuckle their seat belts for five seconds to pick up a toy from the floor of the car. Safety has moved beyond the practical and become an obsession.

Fear is a life-shaping force. If you stepped back and did a thorough survey of your life, you might find that nearly all your behaviors are in some way impacted by your fears. How many hours have you wasted trying to untangle your irrational suspicions? How many nights have you lain awake in bed? How much money have you spent in an attempt to silence your worries?

This is a war we cannot win. Today, we have more precautions and protections than any generation in history, yet people have never been more anxious. This is why God repeated his command to "fear not" throughout Scripture. He wants us to see that the problem of fear can't be solved by our own internal resources. Its roots are too deep. In order to overcome our fears, we must turn to him and receive from him what we cannot produce ourselves.

In Matthew 10, Jesus prepared his disciples to go and preach the gospel for the first time without him. Right away, his message deals with the subject of fear, and like many of his teachings, his comments have the potential to catch us off guard.

> So do not be afraid of them, for there is nothing concealed that will not be disclosed, or hidden that will not be made known. What I tell you in the dark, speak in the daylight; what is whispered in your ear, proclaim from the roofs. *Do not be afraid* of those who kill the body but cannot kill the soul. Rather, *be afraid* of the One who can destroy both soul and body in hell. Are not two sparrows sold for a penny? Yet not one of them will fall to the ground outside your Father's care. And even the very hairs of your

head are all numbered. So *don't be afraid*; you are
worth more than many sparrows. (vv. 26–31)

In this passage, Jesus directly addressed the two great fears that
impact every person, but as usual, his methodology was counterintuitive. The first fear he mentioned was the *fear of man*; he said, "Do not
be afraid of *them*." Who is "them"? "Them" refers to all the people in
our lives who might disrupt our devotion to God.

The fear of man has endless unique expressions, but it always has
to do with our interaction with others. It includes the fear of being
rejected, excluded, alone, or forgotten. It might manifest in your life as
a fear of intimacy or a fear of abandonment. Maybe you can't commit
to a relationship. Maybe you're prone to codependence. These are all
variations of the fear of man.

The fear of man sets us on an unending pursuit of acceptance, but
it isn't the deepest fear in the human heart. Underneath this fear is the
fear of death. The fear of death includes all our fears of danger, lack,
sickness, loss, trauma, and eventually death itself. It produces in us
what the Bible calls a "lifelong slavery" (Heb. 2:15 ESV). We become
entrapped by its power.

This is what crept into my heart on the way to the hospital while
my elbow turned purple. It's what you feel when you are waiting for the
doctor's report about the scan of the lump that wasn't there a week ago.

The fear of death quietly hides in the corners of our lives and then
appears when we least expect it, reminding us of the inevitable: *You are
going to die.* One day soon, your heart will stop beating and your lungs
will stop breathing. Your eyes will lose their sparkle, and you will leave
this place. But where will you go?

No matter how hard we try to convince ourselves that death is natural and that it's just a normal part of life, there is something inside of every person that rages against this notion. Death is not natural, and we don't want to die. We all have our faith and our beliefs, but death sobers us, forcing us to stare into the darkness. What really happens in the moment of death? What will you feel? What will you see?

The Bible teaches that after death you will stand before God and be judged for your life (Heb. 9:27). You will give an account for how you lived and what you did. "We must all appear before the judgment seat of Christ, so that each of us may receive what is due us for the things done while in the body, whether good or bad" (2 Cor. 5:10).

You may not spend much time thinking about it, but judgment day unconsciously lingers behind the fear of death and loss. It is the very center of our most primal fear. What will happen on that day? What will it be like to enter death and stare into the face of God?

When Jesus addressed the two great fears with his disciples, he knew how powerful the fear of man and the fear of death could be. But in the face of their staggering influence, he boldly claimed that there is a way to live a fearless life. You can live above these two great fears, but the way into a fearless life requires a *new* fear.

The fear of man and the fear of death can be overcome only by the *fear of the Lord*. "Do not be afraid of those who kill the body but cannot kill the soul. Rather, be afraid of the One who can destroy both soul and body in hell" (Matt. 10:28). In other words, fearing God above all else is the only way to overcome the natural fears of life. But what does it mean to fear the Lord? It can't mean that we should live terrified of his wrath and judgment, since the next thing

Jesus tells us is that God loves us so much that he numbers the hairs on our heads (v. 30).

To fear the Lord does not mean to be scared of the Lord. Rather, it means to be "overwhelmed with wonder before the greatness of God and his love."[4] The fear of the Lord is the fear of being far from him. It is the fear of wandering from him and the life-altering awe that comes with seeing him as he truly is. Those who fear the Lord cling to him as their very life. There are tinges of terror in the fear of the Lord because, in all his glory, God is terrifyingly beautiful. But this terror is rooted in reverence and wonder, not panic and worry.

When you fear the Lord, you are afraid to stray from him because you have discovered that he is your great shelter. Through the gospel, God has committed himself to you in covenant love, and this promise provides the only safe place for the soul. When his opinion of you matters more than anyone or anything, the fear of man loses its grip. When his promise of eternal life is internalized and believed, the fear of death no longer rules your heart.

> When God's opinion of you matters more than anyone or anything, the fear of man loses its grip. When his promise of eternal life is internalized and believed, the fear of death no longer rules your heart.

This is the only way to overcome the two great fears, to believe that God is *your* Father through the gospel. He numbers the hairs on your head, and you are far more valuable to him than many sparrows. Run to him, cling to him, and turn to him like a child turns to their dad. When you do, his love overcomes fear.

The Refuge

CJ grew up on a small island in the Philippines, and in April of 2022, his hometown was hit by a massive tropical storm. The storm caused mudslides so great that entire neighborhoods were being wiped out, and millions of people were being displaced. As the mudslides rapidly approached his home, eleven-year-old CJ was gripped with fear. He could see them coming, and just before the wave of mud reached his house, he opened the refrigerator in the kitchen, ripped out all the shelving, and climbed inside.

Twenty hours later, CJ climbed out of the refrigerator when it washed up on a nearby riverbank, and rescue workers helped him to safety.[5] Miraculously, he hadn't suffocated or drowned. He had survived the storm. Thousands of people lost their lives that day, but CJ was spared because he had sought refuge in a shelter that was strong enough to make it through.

What is a refuge? It's a safe place, a place of healing and retreat. It's where you run when trouble strikes. Superman went to his Fortress of Solitude. Batman had the Batcave. Even our superheroes have places of refuge, but few people today have learned to intentionally turn to God first when troubles come. Instead, we often turn to him last. After the pills have failed and the entertainments and distractions have ended, then we turn to God and ask for his help. Our first instinct is usually to try to fix the problem ourselves, and once we've exhausted our natural means, we then say things like, "Well, all we can do now is pray."

But this is what separates those who fear the Lord and those who do not. People who have learned the fear of the Lord turn to God first. He is not their "safety net" if all else fails and no other options remain. Instead, he is their refuge—the first place they go when the storm comes.

The theme of refuge appears frequently in the Bible. The Hebrew word for *refuge* means "to flee." It describes a place where people can go in the midst of danger. Think of London during World War II, when thousands of families built bomb shelters in their backyards. As Nazi planes flew overhead, the citizens of London ran to their shelters. These small underground bunkers saved the lives of countless people.[6]

The Psalms in particular frequently remind us to look to God as our safe place. "The LORD is a refuge for the oppressed, a stronghold in times of trouble" (9:9). "As for God, his way is perfect: The LORD's word is flawless; he shields all who take refuge in him" (18:30). Again and again, God promises to be your shield if you will run to him and make him your refuge. "Taste and see that the LORD is good; blessed is the one who takes refuge in him" (34:8).

Probably the most famous illustration of refuge in the Bible is the story of Noah's ark. In Genesis 6, we learn that the earth was full of wickedness and that God "regretted" that he had made human beings (vv. 5–7). When the story speaks of God's regret, it doesn't mean that God made a mistake. The word literally means that God "breathed out strongly." He sighed. He felt pain and grief over people's sin. The human race had abused his kindness and distorted his creation, and this broke God's heart. Because God is both holy and just, the sin of the world required his judgment.

The story tells us that God's judgment would come in the form of a flood. As we saw in chapter 1, God is the ruler over the seas, and in this instance, he used the waters to bring forth justice. In the midst of his wrath against sin, God chose to show mercy to a man named Noah. He commanded Noah to build a giant boat and gave specific instructions on how to do it.

> So make yourself an ark of cypress wood; make rooms in it and coat it with pitch inside and out. This is how you are to build it: The ark is to be three hundred cubits long, fifty cubits wide and thirty cubits high. Make a roof for it, leaving below the roof an opening one cubit high all around. Put a door in the side of the ark and make lower, middle and upper decks. (Gen. 6:14–16)

These instructions are incredibly specific, and it's possible that at the time a vessel like this had never been built. The account of Noah's ark doesn't attempt to answer the hundreds of questions that arise in our modern context, but it does reveal to us a number of important truths about God.

First, it teaches us that Noah was not chosen primarily because of *his* righteousness, but because of God's great kindness. We read that Noah had found "favor" (or "grace") in the eyes of God (Gen. 6:8). This means that God spared the human race as an expression of his love. The driving force behind God's deliverance was not Noah's worthiness, but God's loving nature.

Second, we see that God provides only *one* option for deliverance. He didn't offer Noah an array of choices. Instead, the ark was the only option made available. Noah couldn't improve upon the design, and he couldn't build a submarine or a helicopter. Either he was to build the ark or he would be swept away in the flood. Those were his options.

Noah chose to obey God, and he embarked on the project of building the ark, which took decades. What did his family think? What did his neighbors say? We don't know all the implications of Noah's obedience, but when the ark was finally completed, he and his family entered the boat along with a variety of animals, and then the rain began.

The ark served as a refuge in the storm, and the story of Noah's ark is meant to point beyond itself. Like the bronze serpent, the flaming torch, or the ram trapped in the thicket, God uses this story to make his bigger story of redemption more vivid and clear. How does God plan to save the world from judgment? How does he intend to reveal himself as our true refuge? God provided the answers to these questions in the details of Noah's ark.

Safe through the Storm

The first puzzling aspect of the ark is its dimensions. Why was God so specific about the length of three hundred cubits, the breadth of fifty cubits, and the height of thirty cubits? The early church father Augustine shared an intriguing insight:

> For even its very dimensions, in length, breadth, and
> height represent the human body ... For the length of
> the human body, from the crown of the head to the
> sole of the foot, is six times its breadth from side to
> side, and ten times its depth or thickness, measuring
> from back to front: that is to say, the measure of a
> man as he lies on his back or on his face, he is six

times as long from head to foot as he is broad from side to side, and ten times as long as he is high from the ground. And therefore the ark was made 300 cubits in length, 50 in breadth, and 30 in height.[7]

Augustine suggested that God was so specific about the dimensions of the ark because he wasn't just building a boat; he was building a man. Specifically, he was giving us a picture of a man lying down. The name *Noah* means "rest," and through this story, God is teaching us that he gives favor to the one who will enter and "rest" in his ark.

The ark itself represented a man who would lay down his life, providing a prophetic picture of how God planned to save the whole world from the storm of his judgment against sin. He would do it through a man who would lie down. There were not two or three options for deliverance. There was only one ark, after all. This was the way—only the man laying down his life could save us from the storm.

The picture of the ark as a man points us to Jesus, who laid down his life to deliver us from the storm of sin and death. But the details of Noah's ark take us even deeper into the truths of the gospel. Noah was told to enter and exit the ark through "the side" (Gen. 6:16). It was the only entrance God instructed him to build. When the flood eventually subsided, Noah and his family came forth from this side entrance into a cleansed world.

In the story of creation, the side of the man was the place from which God brought forth the woman (Gen. 2:21–22). He took Eve from Adam's side, providing the first bride for the first man. It was also in the side of Jesus that the soldier pierced Christ with his spear, confirming that Jesus was, in fact, dead (John 19:34).

Why does Scripture specifically mention the side of Adam, the side of the ark, and the side of Jesus? From the side of Adam came forth his bride, Eve. From the side of the ark came forth Noah and his family. From the side of Christ came forth the blood of the covenant, the price he paid for his bride, the church (Acts 20:28; Eph. 5:32). Just as Noah had to enter the ark in order to be saved, so we must enter into Christ, the man lying down, and when we do, he becomes for us our refuge from the judgment of God.

Through the pounding of the storm, Noah's ark endured. It was a strong and stable ship because every inch was covered in *pitch*. God had instructed Noah to coat the ark with pitch "inside and out" (Gen. 6:14). This seems a little excessive. Why coat every inch of even the inside with pitch?

Pitch is generally understood as some type of composite sap used to fill cracks in the boat and stop water from getting in between the boards. In a strange play on words, the author of the story used the Hebrew word *kapar*, which is translated "pitch" in this verse's English translation.[8] The word kapar appears dozens of times in the Old Testament, but this is the only instance where the word is translated "pitch."[9]

Seventy-one other times, kapar is translated "atonement," which means "to cover, propitiate, or remove the consequences of sin."[10] Atonement was what the high priest of Israel did when he made sacrifices on behalf of the people (Ex. 30:10). He covered their sin with the blood of the lamb. The text in Genesis literally reads that God instructed Noah to cover the ark inside and out with *atonement*—which makes no sense unless this ark is intended to be understood as far more than a boat.

Just as this vessel was completely covered in pitch, so Christ was our complete atonement for sin, and he delivered us by lying down in death. According to Genesis 6, the ark had no windows. Noah couldn't look out and see how things were going. However, he could look *up*, because God had instructed him to build a skylight in the roof (Gen. 6:16). In the same way, Christians must learn not to look out but up, and when we do, we discover a refuge from the storm.

When the rain finally stopped and the water subsided, God made a promise to never again flood the earth, and he gave Noah the sign of a rainbow in the sky to confirm his promise (Gen. 9:12–13). The rainbow itself became a prophetic picture of God's plan to save the world. Judgment would not come upon us for our sin. Instead, the great bow in the sky pointed up. God would not fire his arrow of judgment down at the earth; he would fire the arrow into heaven. His only Son would be fatally pierced so that he might justly spare us from the judgment of sin.

The story of Noah's ark teaches us that Christ is our refuge, but what must we do in light of the story? Run to the ark. Enter into Christ. Make him your first impulse in times of trouble, and if you do, he will give you the strength to overcome your greatest fears.

In Isaiah 53, the prophet foretold of God's suffering servant. According to Isaiah, the Servant of the Lord would come and live a blameless life and then die for the sins of the world and bear our iniquities (Isa. 53:4–12). Isaiah described "the man lying down" of Genesis 6, but once the sacrifice was made, God changed his tone and proclaimed the new covenant of grace.

> "To me this is like the days of Noah,
>   when I swore that the waters of Noah would never
>   again cover the earth.

So now I have sworn not to be angry with you,
    never to rebuke you again.
Though the mountains be shaken
    and the hills be removed,
yet my unfailing love for you will not be shaken
    nor my covenant of peace be removed,"
    says the LORD, who has compassion on you.
        (Isa. 54:9–10)

Isaiah connected the promise made to Noah with the future promise given through Christ. Because of Jesus, we will not drown. He has become our perfect refuge who delivers us from every fear. "So do not fear, for I am with you; do not be dismayed, for I am your God. I will strengthen you and help you; I will uphold you with my righteous right hand" (Isa. 41:10).

Who is the "right hand" of God? Jesus himself. He is the one who sits at the right hand of the Father (Rom. 8:34). He is the one who upholds us, and it is from his strength that we receive our strength.

One of my favorite details found in the story of Noah's ark came when Noah finally entered the ark and the rain began. Noah himself did not close the door, and it wasn't Noah who kept his family safe inside. It was God. "The LORD shut him in" (Gen. 7:16). God closed the door behind Noah, and it's God who keeps us in Christ.

This is why Paul could write years later, "I am sure of this, that he who began a good work in you will bring it to completion" (Phil. 1:6 ESV). "He will also keep you firm to the end, so that you will be blameless on the day of our Lord Jesus Christ" (1 Cor. 1:8).

Jesus is the great refuge for all who run to him. And when you do, God himself holds the door shut and keeps you from falling away. A fearless life is possible only when your heart is convinced that the Lord is your refuge. Theologian J. I. Packer wrote, "Your faith will not fail while God sustains it; you are not strong enough to fall away while God is resolved to hold you."[11] He won't let you go, and this leads to a new definition of safety.

The New Safety

What does it really mean to find your safety in Christ? What does it look like to live with God as your refuge? It doesn't mean that everything goes your way or that hard times never come. We are all grateful for the stories of the sick person who is healed, the five thousand who are fed, or the storm that subsides. When the kingdom of God breaks into the kingdom of this age, miracles happen. But not every story ends this way.

What about John the Baptist? He was decapitated because a young girl requested his head on a platter. Or Stephen? He was stoned to death because he testified to the resurrection of Jesus. Was God their refuge too? Psalm 91 describes God as the one who stops the flying arrow and holds off the plague, and this psalm has been a comfort to many. But what about the times when the arrow hits your chest or the plague kills your body?

Didn't Satan use Psalm 91 wrongly when he tempted Jesus (Matt. 4:6)? He treated the psalm like a blank check that promises us freedom from all our troubles, but Jesus did not interpret the psalm that way. If we want to understand the truth of God as our refuge, we must embrace a deeper understanding of safety.

Safety doesn't mean a perfect life. It doesn't mean the absence of loss, trauma, or pain. True safety is not the avoidance of all pain but the unshakable assurance of God's eternal love and protection. We learn to overcome our fears when we realize that every promise from God extends beyond the shores of this life and into the next.

Jesus said, "I am the resurrection and the life. The one who believes in me will live, even though they die; and whoever lives by believing in me will never die. Do you believe this?" (John 11:25–26).

At first, it may appear that Jesus was speaking out of both sides of his mouth. Are we going to die or not? Unless Christ returns in our lifetime, we will face death. But the end we face after death is not eternal damnation. Through him, we have the certain promise of resurrection and eternal joy. Until we believe this, we will always be controlled by fear. But when we do believe this, his life and strength become ours.

> **Safety doesn't mean a perfect life. It doesn't mean the absence of loss, trauma, or pain. True safety is not the avoidance of all pain but the unshakable assurance of God's eternal love and protection.**

God has appointed all your days (Ps. 139:16) and marked out your time on earth (Acts 17:26). Until your hours and minutes on this earth are fulfilled, *nothing can kill you*. Not a single sparrow will fall to the ground apart from God's hand, so fear not. You are far more valuable to him than many sparrows.

Everyone must place a wager in life. You can try to overcome your fears with a thousand safety nets and insurance policies, or you can anchor your life in the love of God and believe that he has a plan. He has a purpose that extends beyond what you can fully see or understand, and he has promised to carry you through to the other side. If this is true, then no fear can touch you.

How will you live in light of the truth that God is your refuge? Wheaton College teacher Clyde Kilby once said:

> I shall bet my life on the assumption that this world
> is not idiotic, neither run by an absentee landlord,
> but that today, this very day, some stroke is being
> added to the cosmic canvas that in due course I shall
> understand with joy as a stroke made by the architect
> who calls himself Alpha and Omega.[12]

The new safety teaches us that the safest place on earth is not the place of our comfort or control. Rather, the safest place on earth is the place of wholehearted trust in Christ. That's true even when the outcome is death, because he is the one who holds the key of death, and he is the one who made a way through death for us (Rev. 1:18). This inner posture of the heart keeps us from the panic and terror that run rampant in our world and steadies us through the floods and the storms.

In his final words to the nation of Israel, Moses told God's people of the trials ahead and challenged them to remain devoted to God. Just before he concluded his remarks, Moses said, "The eternal God is your refuge, and underneath are the everlasting arms" (Deut. 33:27).

To know God as your refuge, you must know him as eternal. He will keep you from harm long after your time in this life ends. A. W. Tozer wrote, "Since God is eternal, he can be and continue forever to be the one safe home for his time-driven children."[13] If you run to "time-driven" solutions, you will never find eternal peace. You don't have to be afraid of life or death, because the one who holds them both is committed to holding you.

"Underneath are the everlasting arms." Underneath what? Underneath your problems, fears, insecurities, and sins, God's arms hold you up. Underneath today, tomorrow, last week, and next year, God's arms hold you up. Underneath *everything* are the everlasting arms. If you can grasp this single truth, it has the power to deliver you from every fear. You don't have to carry the world. You don't even have to carry yourself. God is fully committing to holding you up.

CHAPTER 7

WALKING THROUGH FIRE
The importance of suffering in the life of a Christian

*"He said, 'Look! I see four men walking around
in the fire, unbound and unharmed, and
the fourth looks like a son of the gods.'"*

Daniel 3:25

I'm not the best at fixing things. Recently, I went to a friend's house, and as I walked through his garage, I noticed his pegboard on the wall full of tools. Everything was organized. The screwdrivers were arranged by size, and the power tools sat cleaned and ready to use on the shelf below. It was a work of art.

When I arrived home a few hours later, my eyes drifted over to the tools in my garage. The pegboard on my wall held a couple of drooping hooks, and a large pile of rusted tools sat cluttered on the floor. I noticed a five-gallon bucket overflowing with odds and ends and operating as my functional tool kit.

Later that week, I set aside time to patch a hole in one of the doors in my house, and I found myself once again looking through the pile of tools in my garage. I finally located the spackle: it was buried at the bottom of one of the piles, and I realized that the lid had not been fully sealed. It was now partially dried out and chunky. I found the spackle knife at the bottom of the five-gallon bucket, but it hadn't been cleaned since the last time it was used. My wall patches had disappeared completely, and my paintbrush was full of dust and debris. I sat there on the floor of my garage surrounded by half-broken tools and thought, *What am I doing?*

After forty-five minutes of patching and painting, I had successfully covered the hole in my door, but by the time everything dried, I wasn't sure if the patch was better than the hole. It was so lumpy and uneven that it looked like I was trying to hide a body part beneath the surface. My wife came home, saw the patch, and simply said, "Oh." Home improvement projects have never been a great strength of mine, but this was a new low.

Just as owning a home requires certain tools, so life in general requires certain tools, and as we progress from childhood to adulthood, we fill up our pegboards, collecting the necessary equipment to function in the world. We get a driver's license and a credit card. We get a diploma, sign our first lease, and create our first résumé. We collect tools for relationships, tools for our careers, and tools for managing our money.

Strangely, one area in life is often neglected in our development. Few people collect the tools needed to handle *suffering*.

How do we prepare for suffering? This question gets little attention in our modern world. Instead, we prefer to focus on *avoidance*. In previous generations, avoiding suffering wasn't even possible. At best, people could extend the absence of it for only a few days or even a few hours. Family members would get sick and die from illnesses that are treatable today. Households would run out of wood for their fires and shiver through the night.

In medieval Europe, for example, only half of all children lived past the age of ten.[1] Nearly every family experienced the premature loss of a loved one, and family members were not dying in hospital rooms, but in bedrooms. Today, most ten-year-olds have spent far more time playing video games than they have confronting the reality of death. Avoidance can be a functional strategy for a while, and in our modern world of comfort and convenience, we often convince ourselves that although there is still great suffering in the world, we don't need to prepare for it. *It won't happen to you.*

Along with avoidance, the general assumption of our time is that purpose and meaning in life are primarily self-generated. You have to find your purpose or create it for yourself, we're told. Life's greater meaning is determined by personal taste,[2] which means that "my happiness" now serves as an overarching purpose for life. Even if these ideas are unspoken, they hover in the background of our subconscious, and they're fed to us through the arts, education, and entertainment we digest. For most Christians, living for "my happiness" has largely shaped the way we think about God and faith.

In this environment, suffering is almost always interpreted as an interruption. What else could it be? It disrupts our plans, robs us of our freedom, and slows our progress. When we inevitably experience loss, hardship, injustice, or pain, we run to the garage looking for tools to fix the situation. Tragically, all we find is a disorganized pegboard, dried-out spackle, and a fuzzy old paintbrush. We don't have the tools for the job, and this is when the questions start.

"Why would God allow this? If he really is powerful, why didn't he stop it? The Bible says that God is good, but a good God would never let this happen to me."

Suffering shocks and offends us. Somehow, we found a way to edit out or glaze over the hundreds of places in the Bible that deal directly with this issue, and without realizing it, we rewrote the book. We replaced the massive biblical theme of suffering with an oversimplified vision of the goodness of God.

Instead of thinking deeply about a theology of suffering, our faith often struggles (or buckles) under the pressure of unanswered questions. Peter Scazzero wrote, "Our culture routinely interprets losses as alien invasions that interrupt our 'normal' lives. We numb our pain through denial, blaming, rationalizations, addictions, and avoidance. We search for spiritual shortcuts around our wounds."[3]

Surprised by suffering, many Christians unravel. Someone you love dies in an accident. The relationship you thought would last forever falls apart. Your best friend betrays you. Your life is suddenly redefined by an illness. And you don't know where to turn.

"Dear friends, do not be surprised at the fiery ordeal that has come on you to test you, as though something strange were happening to you" (1 Pet. 4:12). According to the Bible, suffering is not strange. It's not rare or infrequent. Like a hole in the door, it's going to happen from time to time, and it's essential that we develop a functional framework for dealing with the pain and sorrow that come with suffering.

Beyond Simple Answers

The Old Testament book of Daniel tells the story of the Jewish exiles who were taken as prisoners from their homeland in Jerusalem to the foreign city of Babylon. Long before the exile, God sent prophets to Israel warning the people that if they did not repent, judgment would come. He patiently waited for generations, and when they would not return to him, he finally brought his judgment on the nation.

The great empire of Babylon leveled the city of Jerusalem and dragged thousands of Jews from their homes, forcing them into the service of the Babylonian king. Among these Jews were three young men who were given the Babylonian names Shadrach, Meshach, and Abednego. As far as we know, they had not personally disobeyed God or ignored his commands. Their slavery was the result of the disobedience of previous generations, and they were primarily suffering because of the sins of others.

As modern readers, this story makes us uncomfortable from the start. Why did these young men have to suffer for someone else's mistakes? They didn't deserve slavery, did they? Without a robust theology of suffering, we start to assume that God is either careless or unjust, but the Bible offers better answers to these questions.

The book of Genesis describes how God made the world without evil or corruption, but some of his creation rebelled against his authority and distorted the good that he had made. Evil was originally an intrusion upon God's created order, and from the beginning, God promised to one day rid the earth of evil's effects (3:15).

The book of Proverbs teaches that every time human beings break or ignore the moral order that God created, suffering is the result. God is just, and suffering often comes into our lives through our own choices and actions. If you lie to your friend, it breaks down trust in the relationship. If you cheat on your spouse, it destroys the marriage. If you steal from your employer, retribution will follow. For many Christians, this is as far as our understanding of suffering goes: bad things happen because of bad choices. It's often true, but it's not the whole story.

If the problem of suffering were as straightforward as the book of Proverbs seems to make it, then few people would struggle with the bigger questions of loss and sorrow in life. But much to our confusion, sometimes the people who break God's moral laws *don't* suffer, and other times the people who diligently obey God's commands *do* suffer. What are we supposed to do when our situation contradicts the rules?

The Bible doesn't shy away from this apparent contradiction, and a couple of books before the book of Proverbs we find the book of Job. Job tells the story of a righteous man whose children were tragically killed. After he received the news of their deaths, his wealth was stolen, then his business collapsed, and then his health deteriorated. Within a very short period of time, Job lost nearly every comfort in life, and he was left in misery asking the question, "Why?" Job was a righteous man who obeyed God. He didn't deserve to suffer like this.

The famous preacher Jonathan Edwards suggested that, in a sense, the story of Job is the story of us all.[4] Although we might not lose so much in such a short amount of time, we will eventually, like Job, lose *everything*. We will all lose the people we love, our youthful energy, and all our wealth. We'll lose our dreams and our sense of control, and one day we too will have to face the great question of "Why?"

When Job's friends came to visit him, they largely reflected the perspective of the book of Proverbs, telling Job that life was an arena of cause and effect. They concluded that God must be punishing Job for some hidden sin. But this was not the case. Job insisted throughout the book that he was not hiding anything from his creator. He had lived a righteous life. He had honored God, and yet he suffered.

Toward the end of the book, God responded, and his response revealed a deeper level of understanding in the problem of suffering. Rather than directly explaining his reasoning, God answered Job's questions with a series of questions himself.

> Then the LORD spoke to Job out of the storm.
>> He said:
> "Who is this that obscures my plans
>> with words without knowledge?
> Brace yourself like a man;
>> I will question you,
>> and you shall answer me.
>
>
> "Where were you when I laid the earth's
>> foundation?
>> Tell me, if you understand." (Job 38:1–4)

For the next few chapters, God continued to ask questions until the point was clearly made. He wanted Job to understand that underneath his question of "Why does God allow suffering?" there is an even deeper question that must be answered first. The deeper question that we often fail to ask is "Why do you think that God owes *you* an explanation?"

For many of us, our own reason has become the functional god of our lives. If we can't understand it, then it must not be true. Without realizing it, we often assume that God is required to explain his superior purposes to us. Can you see how arrogant that assumption really is?

Where were you when he laid the foundations of the earth? How is it that you have elevated your own reason above the mind of God so much that you've convinced yourself that the one who created you owes you an answer?

If you believe in a God who is required to check in with you and report back to you on all of his decisions, then you have traded places with God. By demanding an answer, you expect him to submit all his reasoning to your level of understanding, but "just because you can't see or imagine a good reason why God might allow something to happen doesn't mean there can't be one."[5]

English author Evelyn Underhill wrote, "If God were small enough to be understood, he would not be big enough to be worshipped." Mystery is an unavoidable part of life. But this doesn't mean that we are left completely in the dark. The Bible presents us with a multidimensional understanding of suffering. Sometimes it's caused by our own poor choices, sometimes it's a result of the choices of others, and sometimes it seems to come out of nowhere. In all these scenarios, God is at work, moving circumstances in accordance with his greater purpose.

> **If you believe in a God who is required to check in with you on all of his decisions, then you have traded places with God. By demanding an answer, you expect him to submit all his reasoning to your level of understanding.**

When Jacob's son Joseph was seventeen years old, he was sold as a slave by his own brothers. He was torn away from his family, brought to a foreign land, and unjustly convicted of a crime. Years later, God delivered Joseph from slavery and reconciled him with his family. When his brothers feared that he would seek vengeance, Joseph told them, "Don't be afraid.... You intended to harm me, but God intended it for good to accomplish what is now being done, the saving of many lives" (Gen. 50:19–20).

Joseph was able to see the hand of God at work even in the middle of the wicked actions of his brothers. His story teaches us that God's plan for redemption and healing doesn't always move *around* suffering. Sometimes it moves *through* it.

In John 9, Jesus was approached by a man born blind, and his disciples rushed to oversimplified explanations to understand the man's condition. They assumed that the man's blindness had to be the result of either his sin or his parents' sin (vv. 1–2). They were using the "Proverbs" level of understanding, which explained some suffering, but Jesus responded with a deeper answer.

"'Neither this man nor his parents sinned,' said Jesus, 'but this happened so that the works of God might be displayed in him'" (v. 3). Did God cause the blindness? No. Did the sin of the man's parents cause the blindness? No. What then was the cause? Jesus didn't tell us directly, but even though God didn't cause it, he planned to use it.

After Jesus said this to his disciples, he spit on the ground and made mud with the spit. He rubbed the mud in the eyes of the blind man and sent him through the city to a pool to wash his face. When the man returned, he was healed (vv. 6–7).

Jesus's deeper answer to the problem of suffering was revealed through his actions with this blind man. Like this man who was born without the ability to see, you and I were born without spiritual sight. The dust of the ground was cursed because of sin (Gen. 3:17), but Christ mixed his very substance with the cursed earth and made a balm to heal our blindness toward God.

Do you see it? God's solution to our spiritual blindness was the incarnation. The invisible God was made visible in the person of Christ. He was the perfect balm, the combination of divinity and humanity. When he took the curse of sin on the cross, he removed our debt and enabled us to be born from above. Just like the blind man, we must walk through the city before we can see. If we walk by faith and not by sight, our spiritual sight is restored.

Renowned apologist G. K. Chesterton wrote, "The riddles of God are more satisfying than the solutions of men."[6] We often want clear, simple answers in life, but God will not always provide them. He will, however, use suffering in the story of his greater plan to reveal his glory and transform his children.

This doesn't mean that he takes our suffering lightly. He doesn't. In fact, throughout Scripture we see that God is both deeply grieved and deeply enraged by the suffering in this world (John 11:35–38). But rather than removing it immediately, he has chosen in his sovereign plan to redeem suffering, using it to ultimately accomplish his eternal purpose. From death comes life. From sorrow comes joy. From pain comes power. Tim Keller called this "the Great Reversal."[7]

The gospel itself is the ultimate example. On the cross, God used weakness to display his might and suffering to unlock everlasting joy. The Great Reversal didn't end with Jesus. Rather, it is *the way* of Jesus. "When Jesus calls us to take up our cross and follow him (Matthew 16:24), it means that to be saved and changed by his Great Reversal we must go through our own reversal."[8]

We must learn to die to ourselves, and as we do, we are made fully alive. We must learn to submit to God's sovereignty, and with submission comes the higher wisdom. Releasing control to God leads to greater self-control, and walking by faith leads to greater spiritual sight. Suffering is not like elementary school math. It's more like trigonometry. Trying to understand it all can feel overwhelming, and that's why God is committed to walking with us through the fire.

Facing the Furnace

The story of Shadrach, Meshach, and Abednego provides a compelling example of how to handle suffering when it seems to make no sense. After being torn from their homes in Jerusalem and forced into servitude in Babylon, these three young men were told that they had to bow down and worship a golden statue of the king. Though faced with the threat of death, they refused to worship the image, and their defense before King Nebuchadnezzar gives us a glimpse of their theology of suffering.

> Shadrach, Meshach and Abednego replied to him, "King Nebuchadnezzar, we do not need to defend ourselves before you in this matter. If we are thrown into the blazing furnace, the God we serve is able to deliver us from it, and he will deliver us from Your Majesty's hand. But even if he does not, we want you to know, Your Majesty, that we will not serve your gods or worship the image of gold you have set up." (Dan. 3:16–18)

They began by expressing the conviction that God was *able*. From their point of view, King Nebuchadnezzar did not hold the power. God did. God is more powerful than empires and nations, and he reigns supreme over all the forces on earth. This is the first essential building block in a robust theology of suffering. God is not weak or incapable, and he is not merely three or four degrees bigger than our biggest problems. He is infinitely bigger, and he holds the universe in the hollow of his hand.

In the middle of a trial, it's easy to lose sight of the infinite power of God. Suffering has a way of magnifying our problems and making God seem small. Do you believe that God is bigger than cancer? Is he bigger than divorce? Is God bigger than financial ruin? Is he bigger than death? Many Christians might give the right answers to these questions, but our faith often lacks the substance and fortitude to act on it when the trial arrives. God is *able*, and this conviction serves as the first layer of a strong theology of suffering.

After these three men declared their belief in God's ability, they expressed their confidence in his *willingness*, telling the king, "He will deliver us." Notice that they didn't qualify their statement with the phrase "if it's his will." There are some things that are left unclear in Scripture, but there are many things that God clearly explains as his will. He has revealed himself as the deliverer of the oppressed, the savior of the lost, and the healer of the sick (Luke 4:18–19). It is his will to save (1 Tim. 2:3–4), his will to heal (Isa. 53:5), and his will to deliver (1 Cor. 15:57).

"The secret things belong to the LORD our God, but the things revealed belong to us and to our children forever" (Deut. 29:29). Many of his ways remain hidden, but he calls us to trust him in the areas of his nature that he has made plain. Christians live in this tension, praying for his kingdom to come and his will to be done on earth as it is in heaven. God responds as we step out in faith. "According to your faith let it be done to you" (Matt. 9:29). The belief that God is willing and able serves as the foundation for our thinking about suffering.

Shadrach, Meshach, and Abednego expressed their belief in God's ability and his willingness, and then they added to this their belief in God's *wisdom*. They told the king, "But *even if* he does not, we want you to know ... that we will not serve your gods or worship the image of gold you have set up" (Dan. 3:18).

At first glance, this might seem like a statement of doubt, as if they were backtracking on their convictions, but that is not the case. A robust theology of suffering requires an understanding of God's ability, willingness, *and* wisdom. These three elements coexist and strengthen one another when they are rightly understood. This allows the "what if" that exists in all of us to be replaced by an "even if."

The three young men in the story were no longer asking "What if we die?" or "What if God fails?" because their hearts and minds were convinced of God's goodness, willingness, and power. They accepted the fact that in this life we don't always understand God's ways, but *even if* we don't understand, that doesn't change the truth that he is good. God himself is enough.

Even if they didn't get to live a long life, even if they never got married, even if they would fail to see all their dreams come true—God was enough. When your vision of God is this big, suffering can no longer control your life.

In a fit of rage, King Nebuchadnezzar responded by throwing Shadrach, Meshach, and Abednego into a fiery furnace. Certainly, God could have kept them out, but he did not. He allowed them to be thrown in, choosing to keep them *through* the fire rather than *from* the fire.

Made Beautiful through Trials

In the Bible, the furnace is a frequent metaphor for suffering. It's a picture of refining and purification, and it's intended to teach us that God is up to something bigger every time he allows suffering in our lives. When precious metals are put in a furnace, they don't turn to ash; they liquefy. With enough heat, the impurities rise to the surface and then the smith reaches down and removes the impurities off the top. Finally, the gold or precious metal is placed in a mold and reshaped into a new image.

As it is with gold in a fire, so it is with us. Through suffering, God "liquefies us," bringing us to the place of collapse into his arms. Our impure motives and desires are exposed in suffering. Our doubts and fears rise to the surface and can no longer hide. Finally, the impurities are removed, and we are reshaped into the image of our Creator.

Paul explained this process of transformation in his second letter to the Corinthians.

> So we do not lose heart. Though our outer self is wasting away, our inner self is being renewed day by day. For this light momentary affliction is preparing for us an eternal weight of glory beyond all comparison, as we look not to the things that are seen but to the things that are unseen. For the things that are seen are transient, but the things that are unseen are eternal. (4:16–18 ESV)

At the time when Paul wrote this letter, he had already suffered greatly for the work of Christ. He had been beaten, imprisoned, and shipwrecked. He'd suffered from starvation and extreme exposure to the elements. If anyone should have "lost heart," it was Paul. But he didn't. Instead, the suffering was changing him for the better.

It was *renewing* his inner self. He was becoming more humble, more joyful, more peaceful, and more loving. The trials of life were causing the impurities of selfishness and pride to rise to the top, and God was removing them as they were being exposed.

His suffering was also *preparing* him. The word translated "preparing" describes a process of cultivation, where God better prepares his children to experience and receive more of himself.[9] God was expanding and enlarging Paul's heart, fashioning him into a new shape through suffering.[10]

Think of this process like the formation of a pearl. A pearl is one of the most valuable objects on earth, but it forms only through struggle and irritation. A particle of ocean debris slips under the shell of the oyster, and an internal battle ensues. The oyster wrestles with irritation until something priceless is formed on the inside through the fight.

The pearl serves as a vivid picture of this life, and it also forms the gates of God's eternal city in heaven (Rev. 21:21). Those who enter his city have undergone the same process as the pearl, and something beautiful has formed through the battle. Earlier in the same letter to the Corinthians, Paul wrote:

> We do not want you to be uninformed, brothers
> and sisters, about the troubles we experienced in the
> province of Asia. We were under *great pressure*, far

beyond our ability to endure, so that we despaired of
life itself. Indeed, we felt we had received the sentence
of death. But this happened that *we might not rely on
ourselves* but on God, who raises the dead. (1:8–9)

Paul tells us that God used the pressure to change him. He was
already a godly leader, but self-reliance still lurked beneath the surface of his heart. The pressure drew it out and forced Paul to practice
a deeper reliance on God. With every trial comes a choice: Will you
obsess over the unanswered questions and self-medicate with distractions, or will you use the opportunity of the trial to deepen your
character and stretch your faith?

Peter Scazzero outlined five different phases of biblical grieving
that are helpful for processing suffering and loss.[11] In the first phase,
we must *pay attention*. This means that we stop and listen to the sorrow and anger that we feel, sharing these feelings honestly with God.
The Psalms provide a helpful template. Many of them gush with strong
emotions and anger, openly expressing feelings of bitterness and dis-
satisfaction (Pss. 13; 22; 69:22–28; 88; 109; 139:19–22). They are so
brutally honest that they might make us uncomfortable, but this type
of honesty is essential for our healing. God doesn't want buttoned-up
prayers. He wants us to genuinely express what we feel.

Second, we must learn to *wait in the confusing in-between*. When
suffering strikes, it can leave us spinning, and this is the wrong time to
abandon God or Christian community. Rather than jumping to rash
conclusions or quick solutions, the second phase of processing grief
teaches us to pause and wait for God. Give him space and time. Let the
dust settle in your soul.

Third, we *embrace the gift of limits*. Instead of fighting against our own limitations, we lean into them. We accept the limitations of our own body, our intellect, our gifting, and our time. God made us with limits, and until we embrace them and submit to them, we can't heal from the loss and trauma we experience.

Fourth, we *climb the ladder of humility*. This means that we surrender to God and his will, giving space and time to the interruptions and difficulties of life and admitting our own frailty and weakness. We learn to speak less and listen more, accepting the truth of God's love for us even if we don't feel it. Humility rarely grows without intentionality, and the fourth phase of processing grief requires that we pursue depth of character over natural desires.

Finally, we *let the old birth the new*. We release our past to God and embrace his future work in us. We can't get back the old life. We can't return to yesterday. Loss must be released into the hands of God, and this final step requires that we choose to trust that God has more for us in the days ahead.

As we embrace God's formation through suffering, he begins to turn the trial into joy. Humility grows, faith is strengthened, and the love of God is made real in us. Like the hidden pearl, the character of Christ forms through pressure and struggle, using disruptions and difficulty to bring forth something priceless.

Meeting God in the Furnace

Shadrach, Meshach, and Abednego were bound and thrown into the fiery furnace, and that's when they encountered God in a new way. Rather than keeping them from the fire, God met them in the fire, revealing in the process something fundamental about himself. He is the God who *enters in*, the one who doesn't just look from afar, but instead responds and comes close. He made *their* problem *his* problem.

> Then King Nebuchadnezzar leaped to his feet in amazement and asked his advisers, "Weren't there three men that we tied up and threw into the fire?"
>
> They replied, "Certainly, Your Majesty."
>
> He said, "Look! I see four men walking around in the fire, unbound and unharmed, and the fourth looks like a son of the gods." (Dan. 3:24–25)

God didn't just meet them in the furnace; he walked with them *through* the furnace. He was taking them somewhere, moving them out of the suffering and into a higher place of freedom and joy. This serves as a great comfort for all those who trust God in the middle of their trials. Suffering is always temporary. No matter how bad it gets, it will end, one way or another. He will come for us, and he will see us through.

God's plan for redemption and healing doesn't always move *around* suffering. Sometimes it moves *through* it.

Just as he appeared in the furnace to save these three young men, it was always his plan to meet us in the fire. Hundreds of years later, in the manger in Bethlehem, he came again. This time, it was not just to save a few but to save the world. He stepped into our pain and sorrow, and on the cross, he entered the furnace of God's judgment toward sin. Because he died and rose again, our guilt before God is gone and we can be sure that we'll never be alone again. God used suffering to conquer suffering, and he still uses suffering today to reshape us into the image of his Son. Through the fire, we are changed.

There's an intriguing detail included in the story of Shadrach, Meshach, and Abednego that should not be overlooked. When they were thrown into the fire, they were tied up, but when they came out of the fire, they were unbound. Through the suffering, God set them free. He used the furnace to remove their chains, and as he did for them, so he does for us.

Through grief, loss, sorrow, and pain, God works on the invisible shackles in our lives. He untangles us and unties us, setting us free from the things that hold us back. We come out the other side unbound. This is the heart of Christianity, that the way of life is through death, and the pathway to resurrection is through crucifixion.[12]

Don't live to avoid every trial. Don't expect an easy, comfortable life. Instead, expect the favor of God in every area and then trust his unseen plan when the trial comes. When your heart tells you that he is far away, remind yourself that he is the God who enters in.

He is never far, and his promise still stands. "When you pass through the waters, I will be with you; and when you pass through the rivers, they will not sweep over you. When you walk through the fire, you will not be burned; the flames will not set you ablaze. For I am the LORD your God, the Holy One of Israel, your Savior" (Isa. 43:2–3).

Right now, we are living in between the resurrection of Jesus and his second coming. The new creation began when Christ walked out of the grave, but the fullness of that new creation on earth has not yet come. Theologians have called this era the "now and not yet." The power of the risen Christ already lives in those who believe. Miracles are happening across the globe, and the Holy Spirit is saving the lost, healing the sick, and delivering the oppressed.

But not all are saved, and not all are healed. We don't yet see the fullness of the kingdom of God on earth. Sickness, suffering, injustice, and oppression still have a foothold. The age to come has already begun, but the present evil age has not yet fully passed away (1 John 2:8). In this "overlap of the ages," God's power is available, but it's mixed with sorrow and suffering.

How should we live in this time of now and not yet? We should walk by faith, trusting him to bring his future kingdom now and, at the same time, "glory in our sufferings," knowing that God uses trials to grow our character and shape us in the image of Christ (Rom. 5:3–4).

Eugene Peterson called this way of living "practicing resurrection." He wrote, "When we practice resurrection, we continuously enter into what is more than we are. When we practice resurrection, we keep company with Jesus, alive and present, who knows where we are going better than we do, which is always 'from glory unto glory.'"[13]

CHAPTER 8

UNION WITH CHRIST
The unbreakable lifeline

"I am the true vine, and my Father is the gardener."

John 15:1

People are still talking about Amelia Earhart. It's been over eighty years since she disappeared, yet it seems like every few years an article comes out or a documentary is released proposing a new theory about what really happened to her. At the height of her career, Amelia Earhart was the most famous female pilot on earth. She was fearless, talented, and loved by the public. And then one day, she was gone.

Did her plane really crash in the Pacific Ocean, or did she land on a small uninhabited island? Did she try to establish radio communication, or were the devices on her plane tampered with? Maybe she was working as a secret agent for the US and was taken captive by the Japanese.

There are more theories about Amelia Earhart than there are flavors of ice cream, but a few things are clear. The US Coast Guard sent a ship, the USCGC *Itasca*, to Howland Island to support Earhart and her navigator, Fred Noonan, from below, but communication between the ship and Earhart's plane was disrupted.

Photos suggest that part of the antenna on the airplane was broken or removed right before takeoff. Without communication between the *Itasca* and the plane, Earhart lost her safety net. Adjustments were made. Weather changed. Panic started to spread as the hours ticked by. Finally, the largest search effort in history ensued, but it seems that no one ever heard from Amelia Earhart or Fred Noonan again.[1]

Life requires connection, and just as a small airplane depends on a radio signal to keep it from losing its way, we all depend on connections to keep our lives on track. Think of the last time you looked down at your cell phone and the top right corner was dancing around, searching for a signal. If you're anything like me, the loss of connection can feel like the loss of a limb.

Pinch a nerve in your neck and you will be immediately reminded of the importance of connection. Even though your brain has over one hundred trillion connections, even a single disruption can be debilitating.

Though connection is essential for almost everything in life, it seems that many of us, especially in Western cultures, are constantly intrigued by the idea of "personal independence." Like Earhart, we appreciate the ship below, but we also want to fly our own plane and reach the finish line ourselves. We celebrate autonomy, individuality, and self-sufficiency, and we bristle at the idea of being deeply dependent on anything.

In the documentary *Free Solo*, rock climber Alex Honnold climbed the face of El Capitan in Yosemite National Park. He took the camera crew along for the journey, which allows us all to watch the climb and get a taste of his experience. Many climbers have scaled El Capitan in the past, but Honnold set out to ascend the 3,000-foot rock face *without a rope*. He attempted it "free solo."

As I watched the film, I couldn't sit back in my chair. Rationally, I knew he was going to make it, since not making it would have probably meant the end of the documentary. But the drama sucked me in. Every fingerhold mattered. Even a slight misjudgment meant certain death. I held my breath as, inch by inch, Honnold did the unthinkable and reached the top without *any* help from *anyone*.

It's hard to see *Free Solo* and not feel inspired. It is the ultimate act of personal independence. The film highlights Alex Honnold's amazing skill, but it also brings to the surface something inside all of us that wants to take on the mountain and beat it. We like the idea of proving our independence and accomplishing the impossible through sheer determination.

But the more I thought about the documentary, the more I saw the mirage. Alex Honnold wasn't actually "free solo," and he didn't climb the mountain on his own.

Consider all the various people in his life who had enabled him to make that climb. His parents had taught him to walk and supported his passion for climbing from the beginning. His climbing instructors through the years had trained him to maximize his abilities and stretch his limits. Honnold hadn't designed the special shoes he wore for the climb that helped him grip the rock face, and he didn't drive the car that got him to the base of the mountain.

On a deeper level, Honnold wasn't responsible for the design of his own physical body. He didn't architect the human cardiovascular system or build out the one hundred trillion connections that enabled his brain to function. He didn't design gravity, and he didn't keep the sun in the sky on the day of the climb. In fact, an attack from a single bumblebee could have brought Alex Honnold tumbling down the side of El Capitan, but it didn't. He was "independent" in one sense, but completely dependent in another.

Even though Alex Honnold's accomplishments are incredible and far beyond my own ability to even begin to emulate, his success was connected to millions of other things that could have greatly changed the outcome. We tend to overemphasize our own autonomy and under-recognize the essential connections all around us. But until we see ourselves as deeply connected parts of a greater whole, we will never learn to live in the power of God.

Growth by Connection

Without realizing it, many Christians today bring our cultural assumptions of autonomy into our thinking about the spiritual life and our relationship with God. We see ourselves as "individuals," and we see God as a second party who can help us live a fulfilling life. We adopt what Dane Ortlund called a "God then me" mentality.[2]

Those who embrace a "God then me" way of thinking hear the good news of Jesus and immediately see it as the entry point into a life of faith. God did his part through Christ, and now it's up to us to do our part. First God, then me.

Christians who think this way might try really hard to be good people and to obey God, but they quickly discover that "God then me" is exhausting. They fall back into the same sins again and again and can't seem to break the cycle. They promise God they'll do better next time, but the change rarely comes.

"God then me" is trying to achieve spiritual change through behavior modification, and it can lead only to self-righteousness or self-loathing. If we convince ourselves that we've been very good and deserve God's blessing, we become self-righteous; and if we consistently fail God and can't change ourselves, then we become self-loathing. Either way, this framework for spiritual growth does not bring about deep inner transformation.

After Christians become exhausted with "God then me," we often turn to "God not me." This second perspective is a distortion of the good news and assumes that God will do everything for us. We think, *Let go and let God.*[3] We become passive in our spiritual growth, accepting compromise and sin. Rather than maturing, our spiritual lives move backward, and we find ourselves more miserable and discontented than ever. "God not me" cannot produce a fruitful Christian life because it undermines personal responsibility.

Most followers of Jesus have tried the first two frameworks for spiritual growth and found that they don't work very well. This leads us to a third way of thinking, which Ortlund identified as "God plus me."[4]

"God plus me" views spiritual growth as a partnership. God reaches out, and I take his hand. God meets me halfway, and I make up the difference. He gives a little and I give a little too. This third way of thinking gets us closer to the truth, but a partnership with God is not exactly what the Bible describes.

The radical truth of the gospel is that God saves us through grace, not works (Eph. 2:8–9). Human effort is not part of the salvation equation. You and I were spiritually *dead* before Christ intervened. Dead people don't meet God halfway. As we saw in chapter 2, sin has found its way into the deepest recesses of our souls. We don't need a tune-up—we need new birth.

"God then me" is growth based on human effort, "God not me" is cheap grace that leads to laziness, and "God plus me" still smacks of earning our way to heaven. So if those are incorrect, how *should* we think about Christian growth?

The only way to grow in Christ is to embrace the mystery of *God in me*. This is growth through connection. The more real the truth of "God in me" becomes, the more his life becomes your life. C. S. Lewis wrote, "A car is made to run on gasoline, and it would not run properly on anything else. Now God designed the human machine to run on Himself. He Himself is the fuel our spirits were designed to burn, or the food our spirits were designed to feed on. There is no other."[5]

What does it mean to practice the truth of "God in me"? It means that we learn the way of the vine.

The Way of the Vine

In his famous farewell discourse, just before he was arrested and sent to the cross, Jesus told his disciples, "I am the true vine, and my Father is the gardener" (John 15:1). Seven different times, the apostle John weaved into his account of the life of Christ moments when Jesus used the phrase "I am." Each time, it echoes back to the name that God spoke to Moses at the burning bush in Exodus 3. God is the "I am that I am," and Christ is the "I am" in human form.

This text in John 15 is the seventh and final "I am" phrase in the gospel of John. The author saved it for last because it is the culmination of all the others. The truth of Christ as the vine is the center of the Christian life and the secret to ultimate joy. This theme can be traced through the entire Bible, beginning in the book of Genesis when God put Adam in a garden (2:8). Adam and God cared for the garden together, but when Adam chose independence from God, he broke their union and was driven from the garden and forced to till the ground outside of Eden. Connection between God and humanity was broken. Sin had severed the relationship.

God didn't give up on his union with humanity because of their sin. Instead, he called out one man, Abraham, and promised to restore the divine connection through his family. Abraham and Sarah had a miracle son, and from this son came a family, which became a nation. As the nation of Israel grew, God called his people "the vine" planted by God himself (Isa. 5:1–7).

The imagery of the vine is repeated throughout the Psalms and Prophets. We read, "You brought *a vine* out of Egypt; you drove out the nations and planted it. You cleared the ground for it; it took deep root and filled the land" (Ps. 80:8–9 ESV).

Israel was the vine of God, but they didn't remain connected to him. God spoke through the prophet Jeremiah, "I had planted you like a *choice vine* of sound and reliable stock. How then did you turn against me into a corrupt, wild vine?" (Jer. 2:21).

For generations, God called to his people to return to him, but Israel did not heed his word. The nation was overthrown by the Assyrians and then the Babylonians. The prophets went silent. Rome conquered most of the known world. History seemed to forget God's call to Israel to be the great vine in his garden.

When it felt like all hope was lost, a baby was born in Bethlehem. The one who was both fully God and fully man arrived as the true and perfect Israel.

Then, before he went to the cross, Jesus gathered his disciples in an upper room and told them:

I am the *true vine*, and my Father is the gardener. He cuts off every branch in me that bears no fruit, while every branch that does bear fruit he prunes so that it will be even more fruitful. You are already clean because of the word I have spoken to you. Remain in me, as I also remain in you. No branch can bear fruit by itself; it must remain in the vine. Neither can you bear fruit unless you remain in me.

I am the vine; you are the branches. If you remain in me and I in you, you will bear much fruit; apart from me you can do nothing. If you do not remain in me, you are like a branch that is thrown away and withers; such branches are picked up, thrown into the fire and burned. If you remain in me and my words remain in you, ask whatever you wish, and it will be done for you. (John 15:1–7)

What Israel failed to do, Christ came to fulfill. Israel was the unfaithful vine, but Christ is the true vine. God told Abraham that through his seed, all the nations of the earth would be blessed. Jesus came to fulfill that promise. He is the channel by which the blessing of God comes to us.

The metaphor of the vine and the branch is intended to communicate the climactic central message of the Bible: *union with Christ*. This message appears on nearly every page of the New Testament and is specifically referenced over two hundred times.[6] It is the great "umbrella doctrine" under which every other benefit of salvation can be found, yet many Christians seem to miss it.[7] Our union with Christ is the channel by which every blessing from heaven flows to us.

> God told Abraham that through his seed, all the nations of the earth would be blessed. Jesus came to fulfill that promise. He is the channel by which the blessing of God comes to us.

Just as the branch is dependent on the vine for life, so we are dependent on Christ. To disconnect the branch from the vine is to cut off its life source, but if it remains connected to the vine, it receives all the nutrients it needs to thrive. Our union with Christ works the same way, and it must be understood on both a "macro" level and a "micro" level.[8]

Identified with Jesus

The New Testament frequently uses the phrases *in Christ* and *with Christ* to describe our connection with God through Jesus. These phrases can be confusing, and it's possible to read the New Testament and miss their impact—or not even see them.

For example, in his letter to the Colossians, Paul filled nearly every paragraph with references to our union. *In* Christ we have redemption (1:14), *in* him we've been reconciled (1:22), *in* him are all the treasures of wisdom (2:3), and now we walk *in* him (2:6). We are rooted *in* Christ (2:7), we are filled *in* Christ (2:10), and we triumph *in* Christ

(2:15). This phrasing continues through the entire letter, yet many Christians today miss the central point of the message.

What does it mean to be *in* Christ? To understand the "macro" level of our union with Christ, we must grasp the concept of corporate solidarity. Simply stated, corporate solidarity is when "a group of people is so identified with one person that what is said of the individual can also be said of the group."[9] Corporate solidarity means that one individual serves as the "representative" or the "federal head" for the larger group.

The story of David and Goliath is an example of corporate solidarity. When David arrived at the battlefield, Goliath was standing before the entire army of Israel. There were thousands of people there, but Goliath said, "Choose *a man* and have him come down to me. If he is able to fight and kill me, *we* will become your subjects; but if I overcome him and kill him, you will become our subjects and serve us" (1 Sam. 17:8–9).

Goliath was challenging Israel to elect a representative who would face him in battle. Whoever won that single battle, his victory would apply to the entire nation. This is corporate solidarity, and when the New Testament uses the phrases *in Christ* or *with Christ*, it is referring to this concept.

Adam was the first representative of humanity. So when he sinned, his sin was passed down to all who were born of Adam. This means that those who are *in Adam* die like Adam. When Christ came, he came as the "second man" or the "last Adam" (1 Cor. 15:45–47).

He was a new representative for humanity, and he died as our substitute on the cross. When he rose from the dead, he began the new era of the age to come. Just as David stepped forward and defeated Goliath, so Jesus stepped forward and defeated death, and just as David's victory applied to the entire nation, so Christ's victory applies to us.

Paul wrote, "For if, by the trespass of the one man, death reigned *through* that one man, how much more will those who receive God's abundant provision of grace and of the gift of righteousness reign in life *through* the one man, Jesus Christ!" (Rom. 5:17).

This is union with Christ on the "macro" level. He is our new representative, and all that he accomplished now applies to us. The implications of this truth are staggering.

> Or don't you know that all of us who were baptized into Christ Jesus were baptized into his death? We were therefore buried with him through baptism into death in order that, just as Christ was raised from the dead through the glory of the Father, we too may live a new life.
>
> For if we have been *united* with him in a death like his, we will certainly also be *united* with him in a resurrection like his. (Rom. 6:3–5)

From the perspective of God, when Jesus died, you died with him. Baptism is the spiritual act of faith that signifies the death of your old self. God took you out of Adam and placed you in Christ. Now your old sinful inclinations no longer have a legal right to dominate you, and since you died with Jesus, the jurisdiction of your sinful nature has ended.

This truth does you little good until you understand it and take hold of it by faith. That's why Paul wrote, "Count yourselves dead to sin but alive to God *in* Christ Jesus. Therefore do not let sin reign in your mortal body so that you obey its evil desires" (Rom. 6:11–12).

We must *count* ourselves dead to sin. This means that we believe and appropriate the truth of our union with Christ at the very moment we are tempted. We don't simply declare, "God, I need your help!" though that's always a good thing to pray. Union with Christ goes further and declares, "I will not obey sin because that is no longer who I am."

Christian growth is not primarily an issue of behavior modification but of identity transformation. As we learn to see ourselves in Christ and consider our "redeemed self" to be our deepest self, the power of Christ manifests *through* us. The power to live a holy life flows from faith in our new identity.

When you sin, you are not acting out of your true self. The bigger this truth becomes in your heart, the more it's proven in your life. That was why Paul told the Colossians, "Therefore, as God's chosen people, holy and dearly loved, clothe yourselves with compassion, kindness, humility, gentleness and patience" (Col. 3:12).

Notice that before Paul told them to act correctly, he decreed over them their new identity. He reminded the Colossian believers that they were chosen, holy, and loved. In other words, they were *in Christ*, and from this new identity flowed new power.

Jesus is our federal head, and our union with him doesn't just change *who* we are; it also changes *where* we are. When Christ died, we died with him, and when he was raised, we were raised with him. When Jesus sat down at the right hand of the Father in heaven, we sat down with him too (Eph. 2:4–6). This means that right now, from the perspective of God, we are seated in heavenly places.

Through his resurrection, Jesus began the age to come. As we explored in the last chapter, we are living in the overlap of the ages. The evil age is coming to an end, and the age to come is already breaking through. But what's important to realize in our union with Christ is that the age to come already lives in you right now. Ortlund wrote that "Christ plunged through death and out the other side into the dawning new creation, and to be 'in' him means that he has pulled you with him."[10]

This is the power of our union with Christ. His life lives *in* you. Spurgeon wrote:

> We are at this moment one with Christ, and members of his body. How could we be nearer? How near is Christ to God? So near are we! Come near, then, in your personal pleadings, for you are near in your covenant Representative. The Lord Jesus has taken manhood into union with the divine nature, and now between God and man there exists a special and unparalleled relationship, the like of which the universe cannot present.... Come near, then, O ye sons of God, come near, for you are near.[11]

Gazing into the truth of our union with Christ is like gazing into the sun. It's so overwhelmingly bright that it can seem too good to be true. But it is true. It's the reason the good news is so good. The "macro" level of our union gives us a new understanding of our identity, but the "micro" level of our union pulls us into a deeper experience of intimacy.

Nourished by the Vine

When Jesus illustrated our union with God through the metaphor of the vine and the branch, he emphasized the vital nature of connection. He also undermined our false assumptions about autonomy by telling us that apart from him we can do *nothing* (John 15:5). The branch feeds on the life of the vine in an effortless, continuous exchange, and this is just how we must learn to feed off of Christ. If Christianity is ever going to work in our lives, we must learn to see him as our life (Col. 3:4).

This is the "micro" level of our union with Jesus. To feed off his life requires that we deeply internalize the truth of our own dependency on him and deconstruct the myth of our independence. We are not "free solo." We don't just need a little boost. Apart from him, we can do *nothing*.

Every motive is tainted. Every ambition suffers from corruption to one degree or another. Either he is our life and we are fully dependent on him, or we are cut off. These are the only two options. When we fight and claw and resist the reality of our absolute dependence, we limit the vital flow of the life of Jesus in us. But when we allow the truth of our dependence on him to redefine us, it leads to intimacy and power.

How close can we come to God? How much of his life can we receive? Paul wrote, "He who is joined to the Lord becomes one spirit with him" (1 Cor. 6:17 ESV). This language is staggering. In its context, Paul was comparing the intimacy of the believer with Jesus to the intimacy between a husband and wife.[12] Just as a husband enters into his wife and the two become one, so Christ has entered into us. Sexual intimacy between a man and a woman is just a shadow of the deeper truth of our union with Christ.

We've been "joined indissolubly with Christ."[13] This union cannot be destroyed or undone. "Our fellowship is with the Father and with his Son, Jesus Christ" (1 John 1:3). Just as the eternal Father and the eternal Son have existed for all time in a sweet, mutually preferential relationship, so now through Christ you and I are invited into the circle. We have become partakers of the life of God (2 Pet. 1:4). This is not just a theological concept; it's an experiential reality, "a union of the soul with God, a real participation of the divine nature."[14]

The very life of Christ becomes our life as we learn to "remain" (John 15:5). Moment by moment, hour by hour, remaining in union means anchoring ourselves in his Word (v. 7), continually trusting in his love for us (v. 9), and keeping his commands (v. 10). As we do these things, our intimacy with God grows and his power becomes real in us.

How much of the power of Christ is actually available? "In Christ you have been brought to *fullness*. He is the head over every power and authority" (Col. 2:10). Because Jesus is our federal head, his fullness is now available to us. That's why Jesus can say, "If you remain in me and my words remain in you, ask whatever you wish, and it will be done for you" (John 15:7).

Union with him opens the door to a life of supernatural power. Prayers are answered. Miracles multiply. The limits of a "normal" life are redefined, and God begins to break out in our everyday circumstances. Psychologist William James once wrote, "Most people live ...

in a very restricted circle of their potential being. They *make use* of a very small portion of their possible consciousness ... much like a man who, out of his whole organism, should get into a habit of using and moving only his little finger."[15]

If this is true of all people, it seems especially true of those who are in Christ. What might happen if we took the reality of our union with him so seriously that it became the controlling center of our lives? The power that shaped the cosmos abides *in* us. We can't be content with only moving our little finger when God has given us so much more.

Daily Bread

The metaphor of the vine and the branch provides a picture of what it means to remain in Christ, but the Bible gives us a second illustration to further clarify the nature of our union. In the ancient Near East, the sharing of a meal was considered a sacred experience. Those who ate together understood that they were exchanging more than just food: they were exchanging life.

When the people of Israel were starving in the wilderness, God provided bread from heaven called "manna." The manna would appear in the morning, and "each morning everyone gathered as much as they needed, and when the sun grew hot, it melted away" (Ex. 16:21).

Through this experience, God was teaching Israel how to live in daily dependence on him. The natural impulse of the Israelites was not much different from the way we think. They tried to find ways to store the manna, preserve the manna, or stockpile the manna, but no matter what they did, it would rot within hours. Instead of allowing them to rely on their reserves, God was retraining their hearts. He gave them the strength they needed in the moment that they needed it. Tomorrow's food was only available tomorrow, and if they tried to access it today, they were left with nothing.

Later in Israel's history, God gave the people instructions for building the tabernacle. This sacred place would become the center of ancient Israel, where God made his presence known. Right outside the Holy of Holies, God told Moses to set a table and put twelve fresh loaves of bread on it. Every seven days, the priests would eat the bread and replace it. It was called "the Bread of the Presence."

The symbol of the bread being placed outside the Holy of Holies taught that God desires relationship with us but relationship happens only as we learn to look to him for our nourishment. He is our daily bread, and if we want to come close to him, it requires that we first feast on him.

The Passover meal celebrated by the people of Israel each year once again taught this principle. Israel was instructed to celebrate the Passover in remembrance of their deliverance from slavery in Egypt. When Pharaoh was unwilling to let them go, God brought judgment on the Egyptians and struck down every firstborn son.

The Israelites were told to kill a lamb and wipe the blood of the lamb on the doorpost of their home. As they stayed in the house under the blood, they ate the lamb together. God's judgment "passed over" those who remained in the house.

The Passover meal was more than a tradition—it was an existential experience. For generations, Israelites were taught to see themselves "in" their ancestors. They had all been slaves in Egypt, and they had all been delivered. To eat the Passover was to participate in God's plan of deliverance and salvation.

This practice was followed for centuries, until the night that Jesus was betrayed. It was the night of the Passover meal, and the disciples had prepared the food in an upper room. In the middle of the meal, Jesus stood up. He took the bread and said, "Take and eat; this is my body" (Matt. 26:26).

I'd imagine that the disciples were a little confused. They had participated in this tradition every year of their lives, and now their rabbi was rewriting the story. It may have seemed that way at first, but Jesus wasn't rewriting the story; he was *completing* the story.

When supper ended, he took the cup and said, "Drink from it, all of you. This is my blood of the covenant." Interestingly, every account of the Last Supper fails to mention the main course. We read about the bread and the cup, but we find nothing about the lamb.

It isn't mentioned because Christ *is* the lamb. His blood was wiped on the doorpost of our lives so that God's judgment would pass over us. He is the lamb that was slain to cover our sins, and if we stay "in him" just as the Israelites stayed in their houses, we are saved.

Christ is also the bread, the manna that came down from heaven. As the body takes food within itself, digests it, and gleans nutrients from it, so we take Christ within ourselves for our sustenance and strength. And just as the manna from heaven had to be gathered daily or it would spoil, so we must feast on him every day or we will starve.

This is what it means to receive Christ as our daily bread. "Your strength will equal your days" (Deut. 33:25). God's strength is reserved for the moment that you need it, and it doesn't come one second early. You can't store it up and save it for later. All you can do is learn to abide in him, trusting him moment by moment for the power you need.

The Practice of Abiding

In order to abide in Christ, we must learn to let go of everything else. This doesn't mean that we don't love our spouse, or our friends, or our career. It means that every love in our life pales in comparison to our love for Christ. Jesus guides us to this place of deep dependence by pruning away the things that compete with him in our heart. "He cuts off every branch in me that bears no fruit, while every branch that does bear fruit he prunes so that it will be even more fruitful" (John 15:2).

The dead parts of our life will need to be cut off, but even the fruitful parts will sometimes be cut back. Growth often means being cut. Pruning is a part of growing. This reminds us that trials and difficulties provide special opportunities to experience union with Christ.

> In order to abide in Christ, we must learn to let go of everything else. This doesn't mean that we don't love our spouse, or our friends, or our career. It means that every love in our life pales in comparison to our love for Christ.

Christian leaders through the centuries have called this inner process *detachment*. Detachment is learning to let go of outcomes and making Christ himself the center of our focus and ambitions. We relinquish control of our life and invite God into the center of our desires. God must tear our fingers off the steering wheel in order to feed us on the life of Christ.

This means letting go of our timetable (Ps. 139:16; Isa. 46:9–10), slowing down long enough to become aware of our inner life (Ps. 139:23–24; Rom. 7:15), and inviting God to uproot the self-centeredness that hides underneath the surface (Phil. 2:3; James 1:8).

Pruning is painful, but the results are humility and joy. Soon the truth that "apart from him you can do nothing" no longer sounds like a curse. It sounds like a gift. As our dependence deepens, our connection strengthens, and the fruit of the Spirit begins to grow. "The fruit of the Spirit is love, joy, peace, forbearance, kindness, goodness, faithfulness, gentleness and self-control" (Gal. 5:22–23). Union with Christ is the sacred connection that leads to the fullness of life. The more dependent on him we become, the more we experience his life in us.

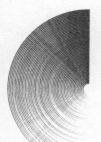

CHAPTER 9

WHEN HE SEEMS FAR
Finding God in the unexpected places

> *"There, above the cover between the*
> *two cherubim that are over the ark of the*
> *covenant law, I will meet with you."*
>
> Exodus 25:22

Planet Earth is a big magnet. Scientists tell us that at the core of our planet there is an ocean of molten iron, and it creates a magnetic field around Earth that extends outward into space for thousands of miles. Without this "magnetosphere," life on the planet would cease to exist, since it shields us from solar radiation and other potential dangers.

Magnetic fields are one of the fundamental forces in the universe. Just as the earth itself has magnetic properties at its core, so the human heart functions as a metaphorical magnet. We are all drawn to something beyond ourselves, searching for a richer beauty, deeper knowledge, higher power, and greater purpose. Most of the time, we end up settling for less.

We become obsessed with a new relationship, or we travel the world in search of the perfect getaway. We grow our careers and our résumés, or we settle down and grow our families. These things are gifts from God, but they don't satisfy the deeper longing of our hearts. In the end, everything we obtain is a chasing after the wind (Eccl. 2:11).

Underneath these great desires, we are ultimately searching for God. "Deep calls to deep" (Ps. 42:7), and God calls to us from the deepest places within. Psychologists refer to this as *intuitive theism*, humanity's primal instinct to look for the divine.

The morning I wrote this, I went to the beach and walked along the coast as the sun was rising. Seagulls hovered just above the water, and the clouds reflected the deep blues, oranges, and purples that come with the arrival of the sun. It was stunning. As I stood there alone, I felt the magnetic pull again. There was something behind the scenery calling out. "Lord ... you have made us for yourself," wrote Augustine, "and our heart is restless until it rests in you."[1]

What exactly are we all looking for? Moses expressed this desire accurately when he approached God and asked, *"Show me your glory"* (Ex. 33:18). David prayed, "One thing I ask from the LORD, this only do I seek ... to gaze on the beauty of the LORD" (Ps. 27:4).

The deep desire of our hearts is to see God himself. We want more than his principles and commands. We want him. More specifically, we want to see his face. Some theologians have referred to this as "the Beatific Vision," the ultimate sight that brings ultimate joy.[2] The desire to see the face of God can be found throughout the pages of the Bible, and God frequently responds to the request. His responses, however, seem to send a mixed message.

For instance, we have passages like this, in which David wrote, "My heart says of you, 'Seek his face!' Your face, LORD, I will seek" (Ps. 27:8) and in which Jesus taught, "Blessed are the pure in heart, for they will *see* God" (Matt. 5:8). Jacob claimed that he saw God "face to face" (Gen. 32:30), and Job declared, "I myself will see him with my own eyes—I, and not another" (Job 19:27).

It would seem from these passages that God allows us to see his face. Yet when Moses asked God to see his glory, God responded by telling him, "You cannot see my face, for no one may see me and live" (Ex. 33:20). John said that "no one has ever seen God" (John 1:18), and Paul described God as the one "who dwells in unapproachable light, whom no one has ever seen or can see" (1 Tim. 6:16 ESV).

In Genesis 3, Adam and Eve heard the sound of God walking in the garden, but they hid from his *presence* because they knew that they had sinned (v. 8). The Hebrew word translated "presence" literally means "face." They hid from his face.[3]

This word appears over two thousand times in the Old Testament[4] and serves as one of the most important themes in the greater story of God. Sin kept our first parents from seeking his face, but the desire did not leave us completely. It still calls to us in the deeper places of our hearts.

If there exists within us such a strong, magnetic longing to see the face of God, why would God allow for so much confusion around whether it is possible? Can we really see him? And if so, how? It seems like beholding his glory is both possible and not possible at the same time. Can this tension be resolved?

Meet Him at the Mercy Seat

Shortly after the people of Israel left Egypt and began their journey to the Promised Land, God met them in the wilderness and gave them a blueprint for their new lives as his chosen people. The blueprint included the laws and commandments with specific instructions for the construction of the tabernacle. The tabernacle had two basic sections: the holy place and the most holy place.

In the most holy place was the ark of the covenant. The ark was a box about four feet long, two feet wide, and two feet high, and it was carried on two wooden poles. It contained within it the stone tablets of the Ten Commandments and other sacred elements (Heb. 9:4). The ark was overlaid with gold, and a lid sat on top of it. The ends of the lid were adorned with two angels (or cherubim) made of gold and facing each other.

This lid was called the "mercy seat" or the "atonement cover" (Ex. 25:17). The high priest would enter the most holy place once a year on the Day of Atonement and sprinkle blood on the mercy seat. It was here that God promised to meet Moses with his *presence*.

"There, above the cover between the two cherubim that are over the ark of the covenant law, I will *meet with you* and give you all my commands for the Israelites" (Ex. 25:22).

The ark of the covenant is an important part of God's redemption story, and it provides a vivid road map to help us understand our relationship with God. Each detail of the ark carries significance. That it was to be placed in the most holy place emphasized its sacredness and the truth that God is holy and cannot be known apart from holiness.

The moral law, embodied in the Ten Commandments, forms the foundation for a holy life.

In those days, it was customary for important documents to be put at the feet of the king. The ark held the law and was a picture of the footstool of God's throne. The invisible God sat "enthroned between the cherubim" (Ps. 80:1) above the ark.

The mercy seat was between God and the law. It was the connection point between God's holiness and humanity's sinfulness. The blood of the sacrificial lamb was sprinkled on the mercy seat because only through atonement could a holy God come near to sinners. This imagery taught the people of Israel that a sacrifice had to be made for relationship with God to be possible.

Imagine the awe and excitement that Moses must have felt as God promised to meet with him above the mercy seat. It seemed as though his request to see God's glory would be answered after all. For years, Moses entered this special place to interact with God. As he approached the ark of the covenant, the room would fill with smoke. Peering through the smoke, what exactly did Moses *see* above the cover and between the cherubim?

By all accounts, it appears that he saw *nothing*. No face. No form. Just an empty space. Certainly, God was present in a powerful way, but for all the amazing things that Moses experienced, the deep cry of his heart to see the face of God was not fully satisfied.

Throughout the stories recorded in Scripture, God often chose to reveal himself in ways that we don't expect. He was a flaming torch before Abraham and a burning bush with Moses. He wrestled with Jacob in the dark and came to Job in a whirlwind. Sometimes he came late, and other times he came unexpectedly. He might appear with a whisper ... or not at all.

Anyone who has genuinely sought after the face of God has had this experience. We are frequently left with shadows and glimpses, but our hearts long for more. There are times when we seek God and, like Moses, find only an empty space. Is our pursuit hopeless? How do we live in the presence of God?

Thankfully, these questions are not new. Throughout the Psalms, we find laments about the apparent absence of God. In Psalm 13, David wrote, "How long, LORD? Will you forget me forever? How long will you hide *your face* from me? How long must I wrestle with my thoughts and day after day have sorrow in my heart?" (vv. 1–2).

David didn't sugarcoat the fact that there was a gap between his desire for God and his experience of God. In Psalm 10, we read, "Why, LORD, do you stand far off? Why do you hide yourself in times of trouble?" (v. 1). These questions fill the pages of Scripture, and saints throughout history have struggled with them.

Maybe you've had this experience yourself, where you prayed for hours, but in the end, it seemed as if God never answered. There was no sign, no voice, no breakthrough. Sometimes, this goes on for days or even years. Why would God instruct Moses to go through all the trouble of setting up the tabernacle and building the ark and then leave him with an empty space?

Why would he put inside of us a desire for him if there really was no way to reach him? Could it be that we've missed something along the way? What if God's silence was actually part of his message? Could the silence itself *be* the message?

Finding God in the Desert

Before Moses ever met God at the mercy seat, he had already met him in the desert. Moses spent forty years in obscurity after he fled from Egypt, and it was during this time that God prepared him to lead the exodus. This extended time in the desert is an often-repeated theme in the lives of those who draw near to God. "Throughout scripture and the history of the church, the desert has been a place of spiritual preparation, purification, and transformation."[5] David and Elijah both wandered the desert. John the Baptist launched his ministry after years in the desert. The desert played an important part in the life of the apostle Paul as well.

Moses went through a host of changes as he wandered in the wilderness for forty years. As far as we know, he never heard God speak or experienced a single miracle during this time, but he did learn to *wait*.

> **Why would God put inside of us a desire for him if there really was no way to reach him? What if God's silence was actually part of his message? Could the silence itself *be* the message?**

As he waited for God in the desert, Moses got married, started a family, and named his first son Gershom (Ex. 2:22). The name means "I am a stranger," which tells us something about the inner life of Moses in this season. He had gone from fame and fortune in Egypt, growing up in the palace of the king, to obscurity in the desert, and it seemed that he was finally ready to confront the deeper problems in his soul. Who was he? Was he an Israelite or an Egyptian? What did he really believe about life, about God, and about himself?

Spiritual director and teacher Ruth Haley Barton wrote, "It had taken a very long time, but finally Moses was able to acknowledge what was underneath the behavior that had gotten him where he was. He was finally able to admit that all his life he had struggled with his identity and he was mad as hell about it."[6]

In the desert, Moses came to the conclusion that he was a *stranger*—a stranger to God, a stranger to the world, and a stranger even to himself. In Egypt, he thought he knew who he was, but the desert had exposed him. God was "deconstructing" Moses's self-made, performance-driven identity, and this deep work would be essential for his later calling.

But the desert didn't just expose him—it also prepared him. As Moses wandered through the hillside caring for a herd of sheep, God was reshaping his soul so he would be ready to shepherd a nation.

The theme of "desert preparation" can also be seen in the life of Jesus, when the Spirit led him to spend forty days in the wilderness and he lived among the wild beasts (Mark 1:13). Perhaps Jesus encountered natural wild beasts, but he certainly came face to face with the inner turmoil that exists within all of us. While in the desert, Jesus confronted the devil. Henri Nouwen noted how "there he was tempted with the three compulsions of the world: to be *relevant* ('turn stones into loaves'), to be *spectacular* ('throw yourself down'), and to be *powerful* ('I will give you all these kingdoms')."[7]

Just as Jesus himself wrestled with these three temptations, so every follower of Christ must walk through the desert. We will all face times when we are tempted to be relevant, spectacular, or powerful at the expense of being humble, submitted to God, and faithful. The desert is often a place where it seems like God is silent, but it's also where we learn that his silence is not the same as his absence. In the quiet, God is giving us the answer.

C. S. Lewis had this experience himself many times. He explained, "When I lay these questions before God I get no answer. But a rather special sort of 'no answer.' It is not the locked door. It is more like a silent gaze. As though he shook his head, like, 'Peace, child, you don't understand.'"[8]

Through times of silence, God often meets us with his "no answer" answer. He is training our hearts to recognize his steady gaze and to realize that we didn't actually need him to speak after all. What we really needed was for him to be *there*, and now that the eyes of our hearts are aware of his presence, *his presence is enough*.

There is a difference between "empty silence" and "full silence." Empty silence leaves us alone and scared, but full silence teaches us to rest secure in the love of God.[9]

Have you personally experienced the place of full silence? You can, but it will require time in the desert. In the third to the fifth centuries, Christians throughout Syria, Palestine, and Egypt fled to the desert for seasons of solitude and silence. They became known as the Desert Fathers and Mothers.

Henri Nouwen wrote, "For them, the word is the instrument of the present world and silence is the mystery of the future world. If a word is to bear fruit, it must be spoken from the future world into the present world. The Desert Fathers therefore considered their going into the silence of the desert to be a first step into the future world."[10]

Through silence and solitude, God pulls us into his future reality. There, he speaks in ways that we will never understand if we stay busy and fully absorbed in the hustle and distractions of life. Before we can "see his face," before we can catch a glimpse of the Beatific Vision, we must find him in the silence and learn to hear his voice even when he doesn't speak.

There's a story in 1 Kings 19 that vividly illustrates the power of silence. The prophet Elijah had called fire down from heaven and defeated the false prophets of Baal, and after his great victory, he expected the people to immediately turn back to God. But they didn't. Instead, the wicked queen Jezebel threatened his life, and Elijah found himself hiding from the queen and on the run in the wilderness.

It didn't take long before Elijah emotionally crashed. He went from a great spiritual high to a deep depression overnight, and before long, he was asking God to take his life (1 Kings 19:4). He was exhausted physically, emotionally, and spiritually, and in his fatigue, Elijah had allowed *fear* to overtake him.

God's remedy for healing in this story seemed to come out of nowhere. Rather than giving Elijah some powerful spiritual encounter, God gave him food and told him to go to sleep (1 Kings 19:5–6). This might sound "unspiritual" to us, but the story teaches that there is clearly a connection between our bodies and our spirits. Things like eating, exercising, and sleeping have a marked effect on the mind and its ability to process reality.[11] Sometimes our struggle to hear God is less about his willingness or our holiness and more about our physical condition. Tired people often make really bad decisions.

After Elijah ate and slept, God led him to a cave, and he waited there for God to speak. "The LORD said, 'Go out and stand on the mountain in the presence of the LORD, for the LORD is about to pass by'" (1 Kings 19:11). The word translated "presence" is the same word that we saw earlier in Genesis 3:8. It means "face." God told Elijah to go out and expect to see his face, which is the deep magnetic cry of every human heart from the beginning. We long to see his face, yet so often it is veiled.

Elijah stood at the edge of the cave and was met by a powerful wind, but the Lord was not in the wind. After that, there was an earthquake and then a fire, but God was not in those things either. Then, at last came the sound of a "low whisper" (1 Kings 19:12 ESV). The literal translation is the sound of *sheer silence*.[12] Elijah heard the "non-response" of God, and this encounter at the cave led to clarity and renewal.

What did Moses do while he was in the desert? What did Elijah do while he was alone in the wilderness? What did David do in the field? What did Joseph do in prison? All these stories affirm the same truth: those who knew God best *learned to wait*. What then should we do when God seems far? Quiet our souls and wait expectantly.

David wrote, "My heart is not proud, LORD, my eyes are not haughty; I do not concern myself with great matters or things too wonderful for me. But I have calmed and quieted myself, I am like a weaned child with its mother; like a weaned child I am content" (Ps. 131:1–2).

David understood that it was his job to quiet himself before God. God often meets us in unexpected ways and at unexpected times. He speaks through words and through silence. In order to hear him and see him, we must embrace the lessons of the desert.

But there is more to the story than just the empty space. God left the space above the ark and between the cherubim empty in the Old

Testament, but he always planned to fill that space through the coming of his Son.

Mary Saw Him

Early in the morning on the third day after Jesus was crucified, Mary Magdalene went to his tomb. She immediately noticed that the stone had been rolled away, and she feared that someone had desecrated the resting place of Jesus and stolen his body in the night. She ran back and got Peter and John, who went into the empty tomb and then returned home.

But Mary Magdalene couldn't leave. She lingered. We aren't told how long she waited, but her willingness to wait is an example for us. Just like Moses and Elijah, she found herself alone, peering into the emptiness, and waiting. Mary stayed there until the emptiness she experienced *became* fullness.

A. W. Tozer reflected on the characteristics of those who personally encounter God. "Something in them was open to heaven, something that urged them Godward.... They had spiritual awareness and ... they went on to cultivate it until it became the biggest thing in their lives. They differed from the average person in that when they felt the inward longing they did something about it."[13]

As Mary waited outside the empty tomb, two angels appeared. John described the scene this way: "She saw two angels in white, sitting where the body of Jesus had lain, *one at the head and one at the feet*" (John 20:12 ESV).

Why does it matter where the angels were sitting? Why would John include this detail? His description seems to reach back into history and connect this event to God's larger story. Remember the lid to the ark of the covenant? When God told Moses to build the ark, he said, "You shall make a mercy seat.... And you shall make two cherubim of gold ... Make one cherub *on the one end*, and one cherub *on the other end*" (Ex. 25:17–19 ESV).

The angels, also known as cherubim, sat positioned on the large slab in the empty tomb in the same way they were on top of the ark of the covenant. Did Mary notice? Had the cave where Christ was buried become the Holy of Holies? In the center of the room was a rectangular box with an angel positioned on either side. Had the empty tomb of Jesus just become the ultimate fulfillment of everything the ark represented?

God was finally transforming the place of emptiness into the place of fullness, because the resurrection of Jesus turned our emptiness into fullness once and for all. Because of Christ, death is no longer an abyss full of darkness and fear. Through his resurrection, death has become an invitation to the greatest banquet of history. It is God's guarantee that he is not far.

Just moments after Mary saw the angels, she encountered Christ, and all of her emptiness was turned into fullness. There was no more fear or distance. She experienced the reality of the Beatific Vision. The ark of the covenant taught us that relationship with God requires a mediator. Between the throne of God and the requirement of the law there must be the shed blood of a sacrifice. Jesus became that sacrifice, and his death connected sinful humanity with perfect divinity through grace.

The apostle Paul wrote, "For all have sinned and fall short of the glory of God, and all are *justified* freely by his grace through the *redemption* that came by Christ Jesus. God presented Christ as a *sacrifice of atonement*, through the shedding of his blood—to be received by faith" (Rom. 3:23–25).

Paul uses three word pictures to teach us what Jesus accomplished through his death and resurrection. First, he tells us that we have been *justified*. This is a legal term, and it paints the picture of a judge who declares a defendant "not guilty." Justification through the gospel is a sheer gift to be received by grace. Because of the cross, you are "not guilty" before God.

Second, Paul tells us that grace brings *redemption*. This is the language of liberation. Slavery was very common in the first century, and the word *redemption* describes someone being purchased and then released from the bonds of slavery. Through his sacrifice, Christ set us free from slavery to sin and death.

The third word picture is the most stunning of all. God presented Christ as a *sacrifice of atonement*. The Greek word used here appears only one other time in the New Testament (in Heb. 9:5), but it's found throughout the Greek translation of the Old Testament, where it's consistently translated as "mercy seat." This is the word used in Exodus 25. "There I will meet with you, and from above the *mercy seat*, from between the two cherubim that are on the ark of the testimony, I will speak with you" (v. 22 ESV).

Why would Paul use this word in Romans 3 to describe the work of Christ on the cross? He is telling us that Jesus *became* the mercy seat when he died. He filled the space that separated God and humanity. Everything that kept us from fellowship with God has been removed, and the resurrection marks the beginning of the new era of grace. Moses looked between the cherubim and saw nothing, but we can look and see the love of God through Christ.

> Jesus *became* the mercy seat when he died. He filled the space that separated God and humanity. Everything that kept us from fellowship with God has been removed, and the resurrection marks the beginning of the new era of grace.

To say that Jesus *became* the mercy seat is to say that he became our mediator. But what does it mean that Christ is our mediator? A second metaphor might be helpful. In the story of Jacob, Jacob fell asleep in the desert and had a dream of a giant stairway that reached from earth to heaven. Angels, who represent the glory and presence of God, moved up and down the stairs (Gen. 28:12–13).

At this point in his life, Jacob was not an honest man. He was a liar and a deceiver, yet God still met him in a dream. When Jacob woke up, he was stunned. He couldn't understand the full meaning of the stairway, but he concluded that God had come to visit him in the night.

The story of Jacob's ladder, this stairway to heaven, didn't get much attention in the Bible until it was brought up again by Jesus centuries later. In his first conversation with Nathaniel, Jesus told his new disciple, "You will see heaven opened, and the angels of God *ascending* and *descending* on the Son of Man" (John 1:51 ESV).

This language of angels ascending and descending is a direct reference to Jacob's staircase. But rather than walking on a staircase, Jesus tells us that the angels are walking *on him*. The Son of Man *is* the staircase that brings heaven to earth and leads sinners into the presence of God. Ancient cultures called this an *axis mundi*, a pathway or connection point between heaven and earth. Jesus doesn't claim to lead us to the axis mundi—he claims to *be* the axis mundi.[14] He is our mediator, our staircase, and through his death, he made a way for us.

Seeing His Face

We began this chapter by comparing the internal magnetic force of the earth to the great magnet that exists within all of us, pulling us toward heaven. God has put "eternity in our hearts" (Eccl. 3:11), and nothing else can fully satisfy. Through his death and resurrection, Jesus paid our debt of sin and made a way for us to enter into the presence of God.

But what exactly do we find as we approach God? Moses peered through the cloud, but all he saw was an empty space. Has the gospel left us in the same place? Can the Beatific Vision ever be realized? Can we see the face of God?

Paul wrote about the topic of spiritual sight in his second letter to the Corinthians, telling us about those who are far from God. "In their case the god of this world has blinded the minds of the unbelievers, to keep them from seeing the light of the gospel of the glory of Christ, who is the image of God.... For God, who said, 'Let light shine out of darkness,' has shone in our hearts to give the light of the knowledge of the glory of God *in the face of Jesus Christ*" (4:4, 6 ESV).

This passage can be a little confusing at first. Paul used a series of parallels, and he first dealt with the problem of spiritual blindness, telling us that it's the goal of Satan, the god of this world, to blind the minds of unbelievers. This blinding keeps people from seeing God's glory, even though it's right in front of them. Paul called the glory of God "the light of the gospel of the glory of Christ, who is the image of

God." In other words, through the good news of the gospel, Jesus has brought God's glory into view.

Next, the phrase "let light shine out of darkness" is a direct reference to the creation narrative of Genesis 1. Paul was connecting the creation of the world with the new creation that has come through Christ. Just as the cosmos was full of darkness and God brought forth light, so our souls were full of darkness and Christ broke in with the gospel.

God began the world with an eruption of light, and he began the new world with an eruption of light in our hearts. The first explosion happened in the sky, but the second explosion happens when we hear the gospel and our hearts are changed.

The phrases "glory of Christ" and "glory of God" are connected to show us that they are one and the same. The glory of Christ *is* the glory of God. Therefore, the knowledge of the glory of God can be seen *in the face* of Jesus. Stated differently, Jesus came so that our deep inner desire to see God could be met. He is the image of the invisible, and we learn to clearly see his face as we hear and understand the good news.

This is what the apostle John was trying to tell us when he wrote, "No one has ever seen God, but the one and only Son, who is himself God and is in closest relationship with the Father, has made him known" (John 1:18).

Jesus is the Beatific Vision. He is the face of God, revealed to us. Later in the gospel of John, Jesus had a conversation with Philip. "Philip said, 'Lord, show us the Father and that will be enough for us.' Jesus answered: 'Don't you know me, Philip, even after I have been among you such a long time? Anyone who has *seen me has seen the Father*'" (14:8–9).

Seeing Jesus is equivalent to seeing God the Father, but Jesus was talking about more than just natural sight. Many people saw him when he walked the earth, yet they didn't see the Father. Satan blinded their spiritual eyes and they saw only a man from Nazareth. But just as God broke in with light at the dawn of creation, so God has stepped in again.

When light first dawned upon the earth, it came through his word. When salvation dawns upon our hearts, it comes by the word of the gospel. It is this *message* that reveals his face to the world. The light of God's glory shines through the gospel, and it comes through the story of Christ's death and resurrection. The story breaks into our hearts and illuminates our souls, enabling us to see the face of God in the person and work of Christ. The more we understand the story, the clearer God's face becomes.

The universal longing for God still exists in our hearts, but the more we understand the gospel, the more that longing is satisfied. As we see and understand the message of his grace, the Beatific Vision gets clearer and clearer. Right now, we still live in the overlap of the "now and not yet." His coming kingdom has broken in, but we still see through a glass only dimly. Our hearts recognize the face of God in the gospel and look forward to the coming day when we will see fully, face to face (1 Cor. 13:12).

John wrote of the day when Christ will make all things new. The earth will be renewed, and the dead will be raised. He will lead us into an eternal city.

No longer will there be anything accursed, but the
throne of God and of the Lamb will be in it, and his

servants will worship him. They will see his *face*, and his name will be on their foreheads. And night will be no more. They will need no light of lamp or sun, for the Lord God will *be their light*, and they will reign forever and ever. (Rev. 22:3–5 ESV)

This picture of the coming kingdom pulls all the metaphors together. The rulership of God, represented by the ark of the covenant, will be at the center of the eternal city. Unlike the ark that Moses built, the empty space between the cherubim will be filled. Christ himself, the Lamb of God, will be seated there, and we will see his face. The Lord Jesus will be the light of heaven. His light broke in on the day the earth was made, and it broke in again on the day he rose from the dead. When he returns, the night will be over, and the full power of the Son will illuminate the earth.

Jesus is the staircase that Jacob saw. He gives us access to the presence of God. Jesus is the mercy seat that Moses built. He atones for our sins, and his sprinkled blood purchased our redemption. Jesus is the face of God that our hearts long to see, and through the light of the gospel we *can* see his glory. When these truths rise like the sun in our hearts, the result is inexpressible joy.

"Though you have not seen him, you love him. Though you do not now see him, you believe in him and rejoice with joy that is inexpressible and filled with glory" (1 Pet. 1:8 ESV).

Sometimes God seems far away, and it feels like he doesn't care. Sometimes we pray and it feels like nothing has changed. Sometimes, like Elijah, we find ourselves tired and alone. Sometimes, like Moses, we spend years in the desert.

In these times of trial, God has not forgotten us or abandoned us. He will meet us in unexpected ways and in unexpected places, and because of the gospel, we can have joy through it all. Mary Magdalene lingered at the empty tomb, and as she waited, Jesus arrived. If we will do the same and learn to wait for him in our emptiness, he will come and fill our empty places with his fullness.

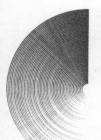

CHAPTER 10

THE FULLNESS OF GOD
Living a life of overflow

*"With joy you will draw water
from the wells of salvation."*

Isaiah 12:3

This book has explored the topic of Christian endurance. Zac Clark lifted a car off his neighbor's chest. Pablo Valencia walked one hundred miles without water through the desert. There is something inside every person that wants to be strong, but no matter how great our accomplishments might be, all our power is fleeting in the end. We get tired, grow old, and break down, and eventually we're forced to confront our own weakness. We want "power for living," but life often just becomes a game of surviving.

The goal of the previous chapters is to offer a road map for a powerful life. Rather than trying to prove that we are strong, we've learned to embrace ourselves as very weak. We've examined our own inner compulsions toward safety, and we've wrestled with the reality of suffering in this life. Through it all, I've attempted to show how God provides more satisfying answers to our deepest needs through the gospel.

The psalmist summed it up well: "Once God has spoken; twice have I heard this: that power belongs to God, and that to you, O Lord, belongs steadfast love" (Ps. 62:11–12 ESV).

God is the great source of power in this world, and apart from him we can do *nothing* (John 15:5). The secret of the gospel is that the more we embrace the truth that we are powerless and receive the free gift of his love, the more we obtain the power of God. To seek a life of supernatural power is not only not wrong—it's essential.

Peter wrote, "His divine power has granted to us *all things* that pertain to life and godliness" (2 Pet. 1:3 ESV). Paul told us, "All things are *yours*, whether ... the world or life or death or the present or the future" (1 Cor. 3:21–22). Jesus said that we can move mountains by faith (Mark 11:23) and that we'll do greater things than he did (John 14:12). In light of these scriptures and countless others, followers of Christ cannot settle for a powerless life. God has called us to live *powerfully*. Nothing else will do.

The story of creation begins with the power of God. "In the beginning God created the heavens and the earth. Now the earth was formless and empty, darkness was over the surface of the deep, and the Spirit of God was hovering over the waters" (Gen. 1:1–2).

These introductory verses give us the great symbol of the power of God. Before there were light, mountains, or men, the Spirit was already moving—and there was *water*. From this first introduction, the relationship between the Spirit, power, and water is established, and water becomes the overarching symbol of power in the early stories of the Bible.

When God brought judgment on the earth for sin, he did it through a flood (Gen. 6–8), and when he delivered his people from slavery, he parted the Red Sea (Ex. 14). As the nation of Israel suffered from thirst in the desert, God provided miracle water from a rock (Ex.

17), and they entered the Promised Land by crossing the Jordan River (Josh. 3). In each instance, water was connected to power.

Water is the most basic source of life on earth, and its power has always been beyond the control of humanity. As we saw in chapter 1 of this book, only the Lord can command the waters and still the storm (Ps. 107:29–31). He is the God of the seas. As God's plan of salvation unfolded throughout the Bible, the promise of God's supernatural power was frequently connected back to the metaphor of water.

Through the prophets, God told us that the day will come when our deepest thirst for his power will be fully satisfied through an outpouring of his Spirit. The prophet Isaiah wrote, "The LORD says ... I will pour *water* on the thirsty land, and streams on the dry ground; I will pour out my *Spirit* on your offspring, and my blessing on your descendants" (Isa. 44:2–3).

Just as water brings life, so the Spirit brings life, and just as water represents God's ultimate power, so the Spirit brings his power to us. The prophet Joel foretold a day when God would bring "abundant showers" and "spring rains" (Joel 2:23), and then he added from God: "I will pour out my Spirit on all people. Your sons and daughters will prophesy, your old men will dream dreams, your young men will see visions" (2:28–29).

Water. Power. Spirit. God's plan is to fill his people with power from the Spirit. It will come like a flood, and it will lead to a supernatural life. The connection went further when the prophets associated the outpouring of the Spirit with the coming of the Messiah. Through God's promised Savior, the Spirit of God would flood the hearts of his people. Relaying from God, Zechariah wrote, "On that day living water will flow out from Jerusalem" (Zech. 14:8), and Ezekiel added, "Where the river flows everything will live" (Ezek. 47:9).

In their broader contexts, these verses, along with dozens of others, connect the arrival of a coming Messiah to the metaphor of water and the outpouring of the Spirit. By the time Jesus began his earthly ministry, rabbis were frequently teaching that the coming of the Messiah would be symbolized through the outpouring of water.[1]

> Water. Power. Spirit. God's plan is to fill his people with power from the Spirit. It will come like a flood, and it will lead to a supernatural life.

Tragically, God's people were not prepared to receive the blessing when it arrived. God warned Israel through the prophet Jeremiah, "My people have committed two sins: They have forsaken me, the spring of living water, and have dug their own cisterns, broken cisterns that cannot hold water" (Jer. 2:13). From this prophetic warning, God wanted his people to understand that a life of supernatural power requires a radically different way of thinking.

A Change in Thinking

The ancient Near East had three basic water sources. The best source of water was a spring that came from deep below the surface of the earth. Springs in the Bible were referred to as "living water" because they were the freshest, purest source.[2] The second-best source of water was groundwater, which would collect on the earth's surface. It wasn't as fresh as the spring, but it was still safe to drink.

The most polluted source of water in Israel was water from a cistern. The landscape is full of massive limestone caverns, and some of these caverns would be dug out and plastered to prevent seepage. The caverns would then fill with water during the rainy season and be covered and saved for a later time. Although it was certainly better than nothing, stagnant water from a cistern was known for collecting sludge, silt, and mosquito larvae. Drinking it often led to people getting sick.

Jeremiah used this cultural backdrop to explain Israel's sin. The first evil they committed was that they stopped treating God as their fountain of life. They were God's special people, and he had promised to provide for them, protect them, and shepherd them. Israel, in response, had promised to live in wholehearted dependence on him. This was "their glory" (Jer. 2:11 ESV).

To live from "the spring of living water" meant to live every day from God's strength. This phrase describes the type of life that we have studied in this book. It's a life that's lived from a place of deep inner dependence on God, where he is treated as the great provider and we are safe "in Christ" connected to the vine, never alone, even in the desert. All of the truths that we've explored so far in this book build *in us* a framework for endurance. We learn to walk by faith and not by sight and find our deepest joy in the sight of God's face, revealed in the gospel.

But rather than acknowledging their own weakness and turning to him for strength, Jeremiah tells us that Israel looked to other sources, namely themselves. This was their second sin: "cistern thinking."

Compared to a spring, cisterns were incredibly shallow. They didn't go down as deep as the landscape required in order to find fresh water. The cistern had no deeper source, just as those who fall into the trap of "cistern thinking" fail to *deeply* consider and apply the truths of God.

We are all susceptible to cistern thinking. It's easy to skim through the content in this book and read about the truths of the gospel but still never drive them down into our hearts. We live in a generation that has become especially adept at learning facts without ever applying truth. Deep application requires deep thought, but the discipline of deep thought is becoming more and more rare.[3]

If we can't understand something in five minutes or less, we often give up or just move on. Journalist Nicholas Carr wrote about this cultural shift away from deep thinking: "Once I was a scuba diver in the sea of words. Now I zip along the surface like a guy on a Jet Ski."[4] Cistern thinking leads to shallow convictions, and when these convictions are tested, they rarely hold up under the storms of life.

In his book *Resilient,* John Eldredge outlined the three levels of depth that exist within all of us.[5] The first level he called "the Shallows." This includes all the distractions and interruptions that pass through our minds every day as we are bombarded with advertisements, social media feeds, and interruptions moment by moment. Too many people spend their entire lives trapped at this level and never learn to make space for any deeper thought. We feed off the constant distractions, and then we wonder why God seems so distant. But God rarely meets us in the Shallows. In order to find him, we must learn to go deeper.

Beneath the Shallows lie "the Midlands." This second level includes all the small fears that scurry around in our minds each day, plus the long-term plans that define the trajectories of our lives. What if you never get promoted? What if you never get married? What if you're diagnosed with an illness? What if someone you love is taken from you? If the Shallows distract us moment by moment, then the Midlands keep us awake at night.

Underneath these two levels of thinking lie "the Depths," and it's in the Depths that we learn to meet with God. This is the place of stillness and waiting. To reach the Depths takes time, reflection, contemplation, and focus. Cistern thinking is the undisciplined tendency to avoid the Depths in favor of the Shallows and the Midlands. When we do this, we forfeit the power of God.

A cistern is not only shallow, it's also polluted. Maybe the most dangerous pollutant in a spiritual cistern is self-effort. In ancient Israel, the cistern represented humanity's solution to avoid reliance on God. If they could build reliable cisterns, then they would no longer need to pray and trust God for rain.

The cistern relies on my supply, while the spring depends on God's supply. It doesn't take long before cistern thinking leads to small thinking. We try to hold on to what we have and protect our resources, afraid to share with others. All the water in a cistern eventually becomes stagnant, and a life marked by self-effort always becomes stagnant as well. We discover that without God we lack purpose, meaning, and direction. We may have a lot of water stored up for the future, but our hearts remain empty and thirsty.

Cistern thinking is so tempting because it allows us to maintain a sense of control and requires little to no faith in God. A man with his cistern full might feel like he no longer needs to pray for rain or dig deep to find a spring. The cistern represents a false security in "self," but it always fails in the end. Jeremiah tells us that the water leaks out.

This prophetic warning contrasts two opposing ways of life. The cistern represents the power of *me*. The spring represents the power of *God*. One way leads to a shallow, polluted life, while the other way leads to an endless supply. Breaking out of cistern thinking is not easy, and it requires far more than a choice of the will. We must personally encounter God in order to see him as our endless supply and live our lives from his fullness.

The Meeting at the Well

The metaphor of water meandered like a river through the Old Testament, but the implications of the metaphor were not made clear until Jesus arrived. In John chapter 4, Jesus traveled through Samaria, and when he reached Jacob's well, he sent his disciples into the nearby town to buy food. While he waited there alone, he met a Samaritan woman.

The setting of this story was very important. The well was near the base of Mount Gerizim, which held a special place in Israel's history. When Joshua first led the nation into the Promised Land, they were instructed to climb to the top of Mount Gerizim and speak a blessing (Deut. 11:29). The place became known as "the mount of blessing," and it represented the place of fulfillment where all God's promises came to pass. Israel had wandered in the wilderness for forty years. But when they were standing on Mount Gerizim, the promise of blessing could be seen.

Centuries after Joshua, division arose between northern and southern Israel, and the Samaritans in the north built a second temple. The location they chose was the top of Mount Gerizim. They claimed that the Jerusalem temple was no longer needed for worship, and this led to a bitter cultural feud between the Jews and Samaritans. And at the center of the feud was the mountain.

Jesus chose this controversial place to bring clarity to the ancient metaphor of water and his mission as the Messiah. At the base of the mountain, the well served as a central gathering place for the community. In Jewish tradition, a well holds great significance. In the story of Abraham and Isaac, for example, God instructed Abraham to send his servant on a mission to find Isaac's wife, and the entire interaction played out around a well. When they met at the well, it was revealed that Rebekah was God's choice for Abraham's son (Gen. 24).

A generation later, Jacob met his wife at a well, repeating the same pattern established with Isaac (Gen. 29). The man arrived. He met the maiden. Water was drawn. She returned to her family. The two were wed.

Before the exodus, Moses met his wife at a well, and the same story played out in a slightly different context (Ex. 2).

Through each of these stories, the pattern is intentional. Theologians call this a "type scene." In type scenes, the same basic elements appear again and again through the biblical narrative with subtle differences, each time pointing to a larger message.

This particular type scene has four distinct parts. First, a man arrives at a well from a distant land. He's tired from his long journey and stops at the well to rest. Second, the man meets a maiden, and as they speak to each other, water is drawn. Third, the maiden rushes home and returns to invite the man to stay with her family. Last, the man accepts the invitation, and the two fall in love and are betrothed to be married.

The storyline of this type scene was known by Jews at the time of Jesus, and John 4 records Jesus's interaction with the woman at the well in the same format. The author used key phrases in the beginning of his account to make the connection. He mentioned that Jesus was "tired from his journey," just as the other stories did, and then the woman came to "draw water." The man asked the maiden for a drink, and water was drawn. The story seems to follow the classic type scene storyline. However, some of the details are shockingly out of place.

The woman whom Jesus met at the well was not a fair maiden but a sinful Samaritan. Isaac found a bride, Jacob found a bride, Moses found a bride, but Jesus found a sinner. Jewish men generally wouldn't speak to a Samaritan woman, and a woman like this was often considered to be in a continual state of ritual uncleanness.[6]

Surprisingly, Jesus struck up a conversation, offering her "living water." This phrase was a reference to Jeremiah's prophecy, comparing the living water from the spring to the polluted water of the cistern. How could Jesus offer the living water of God's endless supply to a Samaritan woman? Notice how the type scene played out.

The man arrived at the well, tired from his long journey, and the conversation between him and the maiden turned to the drawing of water. When the Samaritan woman questioned Jesus about his offer of living water, he took the conversation even deeper and made one of the greatest promises in all of Scripture: "Jesus answered, 'Everyone who drinks this water will be thirsty again, but whoever drinks the water I give them will *never thirst*. Indeed, the water I give them will become *in* them a spring of water welling up to eternal life" (John 4:13–14).

Jesus offered this woman *power for living*—a well that would never run dry. He promised ultimate satisfaction for her heart's deepest thirst. New Testament scholar Andreas Köstenberger wrote that, with these words, Jesus "inaugurates the age of God's abundance. Jesus's offer of living water signals the reversal of the curse and the bareness that are characteristic of the old fallen world."[7]

The first person to receive this offer from Jesus in the gospel of John was the Samaritan woman, because through this interaction he was rewriting the entire story of humanity. The woman didn't seem to know what to do with the words of Jesus, and before she could say much, Jesus exposed the secrets of her heart by asking her to go and get her husband.

She informed him that she had no husband, and Jesus responded, "You are right when you say you have no husband. The fact is, you have had *five* husbands, and the man you now have is not your husband" (John 4:17–18).

Five different husbands? This woman's life was marked by divorce, fornication, and adultery. She had been unfaithful for years, and now her sin was exposed before Jesus. But just when we expect lightning to strike and judgment to fall, Jesus once again did what we least expect.

"The woman said, 'I know that Messiah' (called Christ) 'is coming. When he comes, he will explain everything to us.' Then Jesus declared, 'I, the one speaking to you—*I am he*'" (John 4:25–26).

Jesus revealed his true identity to this unfaithful woman, and it was the first time that he directly told anyone that he was the Messiah. He hadn't told his disciples, the religious leaders, or even his mother. Instead, he chose the sinful Samaritan woman at the well to be the first person to hear these words. She ran back to her village, telling everyone, and soon the people asked Jesus to stay with them.

The type scene is complete. The man came to the well, tired from his journey. He met the maiden, and they spoke with each other. Water was drawn. The maiden rushed home to tell her family and invited the man to stay. But this is where the parallel seems to end. The final stage of the type scene doesn't make any sense in the story of Jesus. In all of the other accounts of meetings at a well, the man and the woman were married, but Jesus didn't marry the Samaritan woman. Why, then, would he follow the ancient type scene? What is he trying to teach us?

The story is teaching us the gospel. He is the Son of God who came to earth in search of his bride. When he arrived, he found her just like the Samaritan woman, broken and sinful, far from God and entangled with many other lovers.

The woman at the well had already had five husbands, and she wasn't even married to her sixth partner. This would make Jesus the *seventh* man in her life. God created the earth in seven days, and the seventh day was set apart as the Sabbath. It was the day of rest because the work of God was complete. In the Bible, the number seven represents completion.

The story of the woman at the well is intended to teach us how God completes his work of salvation *in* us. Just as he came to find this woman, so he came to find us. Just as he confronted her sin, so he confronts our sin—and then reveals himself as Savior. And the same offer of "living water" he made to her extends to us as well.

The story of the woman at the well is intended to answer the great question of our hearts: How can we live a life of *fullness*? How can our deepest thirst in life be satisfied? The answer is stunning. It's the missing piece of the story. *Jesus marries us.*

Isaac married Rebekah after the well. Jacob married Rachel after the well. Moses married Zipporah after the well. The wedding is missing from the woman at the well story because it's the whole point *of* the story. Through the gospel, Jesus takes us as his bride.

Marriage, even in all its beauty, is itself still a shadow of this greater reality. That's why Paul wrote, "'Therefore a man shall leave his father and mother and hold fast to his wife, and the two shall become one flesh.' This mystery is profound, and I am saying that *it refers to Christ and the church*" (Eph. 5:31–32 ESV).

> How can we live a life of *fullness*? How can our deepest thirst in life be satisfied? The answer is stunning. It's the missing piece of the story. *Jesus marries us.*

Marriage with Jesus—this is the greatest reality of life, and this is how he intends to fill you with his power. His life in you; your life in him. Nothing can separate you from his love because now the "well" lives *in* you. How do we learn to access the overflow of his power in our lives? To teach us this, John 7 recounts the story of the water-pouring ceremony during the Feast of Tabernacles.

Come and Drink

The Jewish historian Josephus called the Feast of Tabernacles "the greatest and holiest feast of the Jews."[8] It was held in mid-autumn every year, and it lasted for seven days. The celebration was originally instated to remember God's faithfulness during Israel's years of wandering in the desert after the exodus. It also became a celebration of the harvest season. One of the bigger highlights of the feast was the water-pouring ceremony.

For seven days, the priests would march through Jerusalem and pour water out at the base of the altar in the temple, recalling God's miraculous provision of water during the years in the wilderness. Thousands of Israelites gathered for this part of the ceremony, with everything culminating on the final day.

On the seventh day, the water would be poured out, and the nation would pray for God's future provision. Their prayers would focus on the promise of a coming Messiah and their deliverance from all oppression. Just as Jesus was the "seventh man" with the woman at the well, in this story, Jesus chose the seventh day of the festival to make himself known.

"On the last and greatest day of the festival, Jesus stood and said in a loud voice, 'Let anyone who is thirsty come to me and drink. Whoever believes in me, as Scripture has said, rivers of living water will flow from *within* them'" (John 7:37–38).

I imagine this declaration catching the attention of the masses who had gathered. Jesus didn't restrict his offer to the Jew or to the spiritually elite. He invited "anyone" who was thirsty. Martyn Lloyd-Jones wrote, "The most vital question to ask about all who claim to be Christian is this: have they a soul thirst for God?"[9] The thirsty are satisfied, but the spiritually complacent are left thirsty. We find satisfaction only when we learn to drink Christ *himself.* His message is "come to *me* and drink."

Jesus *is* the water, and "drinking him" is the secret to a life of power. Drink his promises and his accomplishments. Drink his love and his pledge of marriage. Drink in all the truth explored in this book.

He is the one who walked between the pieces and made a covenant with Abraham. He is the ram who was caught in the thicket and who became the substitute for Isaac. He is the ark that Noah climbed into and found ultimate safety from the storm outside. He is the serpent on the pole in the wilderness. When we look to him, we are healed. He is the man who met Shadrach, Meshach, and Abednego in the fiery furnace and brought them out unbound. He is the vine that has become our lifeline. He is the one whose face fills the empty space above the ark of the covenant between the cherubim.

When the disciples found themselves overwhelmed by the hurricane, Jesus spoke to the storm and commanded it to cease. This led to the great question that unlocks the power of God: *"Who is this?"* (Mark 4:41). Answer it rightly, and your life will overflow with his power. Jesus told the crowd in John 7 to drink *him* and then declared, "Whoever believes in me, as Scripture has said, rivers of living water will flow from within them" (v. 38).

It appears that Jesus was quoting the Old Testament, but the strange thing about this Old Testament quote is that it's *not* an Old Testament quote. The statement referenced by Jesus doesn't occur anywhere in the Old Testament. Why would he say "as Scripture has said" and then not quote Scripture?

Maybe as Jesus said this in front of all the people gathered for the feast, some of the religious leaders started snickering under their breath. Jesus hadn't gone to their religious schools, and it seemed that he had misquoted the Scriptures.

But his words were not a mistake. Jesus did not intend to quote *a* scripture, he intended to quote *every* scripture. He was bringing the metaphor of water that ran through the entire Old Testament to its ultimate completion *in* him, revealing himself as the great fulfillment to every one of God's promises. He was quoting Isaiah 58, Proverbs 4, Zechariah 14, and Psalm 77 all at once. He was quoting Ezekiel 36, Joel 3, Amos 9, and Jeremiah 2. Jesus wasn't just referencing a single Bible passage, "but rather the entire matrix of scriptural expectations associated with the eschatological abundance."[10]

Jesus is our fullness, and the ramifications of that fact might be the most astounding part of all. The river no longer comes *to* us. Now, through the gospel, it comes *from* us. The phrase translated "from within" in John 7:38 is connected in the original language to the phrase used in John 19:34, when the soldier pierced Jesus's side on the cross. John linked these two passages through this phrase. On the cross, the blood and water flowed out "from within Jesus" and because of this, his living water now flows out from within *you*.

We saw earlier in this book how Christ being pierced in his side connected back to Noah exiting the ark from the side. Just as God formed Eve from the side of Adam, so Christ delivered us from the flood of sin and death, forming us into his eternal Eve. The result is a new Spirit-filled humanity.

What did Jesus mean by his statements in John 7? "By this he meant the Spirit, whom those who believed in him were later to receive. Up to that time the Spirit had not been given, since Jesus had not yet been glorified" (v. 39).

After Christ rose from the dead, he told his disciples to wait in Jerusalem for the coming of the Spirit, and on the Day of Pentecost the Holy Spirit filled the disciples in the upper room. When Peter stood up to explain this phenomenon to the crowd, he immediately turned to the words of the prophet Joel.

"This is what was spoken by the prophet Joel: 'In the last days, God says, I will *pour out* my Spirit on *all* people'" (Acts 2:16–17). The story has come full circle, and the door to the power of God has been thrown open for us. You can now experience *his* fullness in you.

The Fullness of God

Jesus is the incarnate God, the second person of the Trinity, and the exact representation of God's nature. "For God was pleased to have all his fullness dwell in him" (Col. 1:19). "In Christ all the fullness of the Deity lives in bodily form" (Col. 2:9). Through the gospel, his Spirit has come into covenant union with us, and in this sense, the fullness of God dwells in us through him. "In Christ you have been brought to fullness" (Col. 2:10). "From his fullness we have all received, grace upon grace" (John 1:16 ESV).

The New Testament teaches that we have God's fullness through Christ, but how do we experience it? Jesus promised that we would receive power when the Holy Spirit comes upon us (Acts 1:8), and a life full of the Spirit is one of personal, tangible experience. It's not enough to mentally accept the idea. It must come home to us. We can't earn the filling of the Holy Spirit, but we must humbly and diligently seek it like a child seeks his father for a promised gift (Luke 11:13). As we seek him, Jesus promises to fill us.

According to the New Testament, his power manifests in us in a variety of ways. Through the Holy Spirit, God gives us power to overcome sinful temptation (Gal. 5:16) and break the stronghold of condemnation in our minds (Rom. 8:1–2). He gives us power to cultivate a life full of peace (Rom. 8:6) and experience intimacy with God (2 Cor. 13:14). The Holy Spirit empowers us to share about Christ with boldness (Acts 4:31) and operate in supernatural gifts and miracles (1 Cor. 12:7–10).

All of this can become a reality in our lives as we ask, seek, and knock. The gift of God's power is by *grace*. We don't earn it through good works or anything else. All followers of Jesus have the indwelling Holy Spirit, but the full experience of his power is reserved for those who seek him for his fullness.

Paul's prayer in Ephesians 3 gives us a glimpse into the center of this concept of "the fullness of God."

> For this reason I kneel before the Father, from whom every family in heaven and on earth derives its name. I pray that out of his glorious riches he may strengthen you with power through his Spirit in your inner being, so that Christ may dwell in your hearts through faith. And I pray that you, being rooted and established in love, may have power, together with all the Lord's holy people, to grasp how wide and long and high and deep is the love of Christ, and to know this love that surpasses knowledge—that you may be filled to the measure of all the fullness of God. (vv. 14–19)

Notice how Paul connected multiple themes: power, fullness, strength, and love. The strength of God comes from his Spirit *in* us. Paul called this our "inner being." It doesn't come to us through the Shallows or the Midlands. To live in the fullness of God's power requires going into the Depths.

The deep cry of Paul's prayer was not that we just gain more knowledge, but that we go past knowledge into real experience. Paul was asking God for a miracle to take place. He was begging God to take the knowledge in our heads and drive it into our hearts until it changes the way we see every moment of every day.

Specifically, Paul's prayer was that the *love of Christ* would become the foundation of our lives, so much so that it would pass through the realm of ideas and into the core functions of the heart. His love must redefine us entirely. Paul connected God's fullness to the width, length, height, and depth of the love of Christ because he wanted us to interpret the idea of God's fullness through the lens of his great love for us.

When the love of Christ drives you, lifts you, thrills you, and fills you, you have reached the fullness of God. When his love is bigger than your problems, passions, fears, ambitions, heartache, worries, pleasures, and dreams, you have reached the fullness of God. Stated another way, the fullness of God is everything that God gives us through our mediator, Jesus. To see his love, know his love, and live from his love is to experience his fullness.

In the four gospel accounts of the life of Christ—Matthew, Mark, Luke, and John—there is only one place where Jesus pulls back the veil and reveals to us the center of his own heart.[11] Christ is many things: powerful, holy, just, and righteous. He is full of wisdom, knowledge, and truth. But when Jesus gives us the one glimpse into the center of his personality, he says, "Come to me, all you who are weary and burdened, and I will give you rest. Take my yoke upon you and learn from me, for *I am gentle and humble in heart*, and you will find rest for your souls. For my yoke is easy and my burden is light" (Matt. 11:28–30).

He wants us to come, and he wants to give us rest. He's not disappointed or surprised by our weakness. Rather, he is glorified when weak people are made strong through him. Jesus tells us that he is "gentle," and this reveals his temperament toward sinners. He tells us that he's "humble," and this means he is available and accessible to us. Both gentleness and humility are characteristics of love, and it's here that we find the real secret of great endurance.

None of our strength can come through self-effort or human will, but supernatural endurance comes to the heart of the one who knows he is greatly loved. Love endures *all things* (1 Cor. 13:7), and we endure all things as we remain in him.

Inside you is a spring of living water, an unending reservoir of divinity, the very life of God in the soul. Draw near to the well of salvation (Isa. 12:3). Drink *him*. Your bridegroom will meet you there at the well and fill you with his love.

NOTES

Introduction

1. Dan Witters, "U.S. Depression Rates Reach New Highs," Gallup, May 17, 2023, https://news.gallup.com/poll/505745/depression-rates-reach-new-highs.aspx; and Renee D. Goodwin, et al., "Trends in Anxiety among Adults in the United States, 2008–2018," *Journal of Psychiatric Research*, vol. 130 (Nov. 2020), 441–46.

2. Thomas Howard, *Chance or the Dance? A Critique of Modern Secularism*, 2nd ed. (San Francisco: Ignatius Press, 2018), 84.

Chapter 1: Adjusting Expectations

1. Jake Furr, "Ohio High School Football Player, 16, Lifts Car Off His Neighbor's Chest, Saves Man's Life," *USA Today*, September 25, 2019, www.usatoday.com/story/sports/highschool/2019/09/25/ohio-high-school-football-player-lifts-car-off-neighbor-chest/2443161001/.

2. James R. Edwards, *The Gospel according to Mark*, The Pillar New Testament Commentary (Grand Rapids, MI: Eerdmans, 2002), 148–49.

3. Edwards, *Gospel according to Mark*, 151.

4. G. K. Beale and D. A. Carson, eds., *Commentary on the New Testament Use of the Old Testament* (Grand Rapids, MI: Baker Academic, 2007), 308.

5. Edwards, *Gospel according to Mark*, 152.

6. William Cowper, "God Moves in a Mysterious Way," hymn (1774).

Chapter 2: The Weakness Paradox

1. Alex Hutchinson, *Endure: Mind, Body and the Curiously Elastic Limits of Human Performance* (New York: HarperCollins, 2018), 158.

2. Hutchinson, *Endure*, 159.

3. Steven M. Southwick and Dennis S. Charney, *Resilience: The Science of Mastering Life's Greatest Challenges* (Cambridge, UK: Cambridge University Press, 2018), 8.

4. Angela Duckworth, *Grit: The Power of Passion and Perseverance* (New York: Scribner, 2016), 8.

5. John Eldredge, *Resilient: Restoring Your Weary Soul in These Turbulent Times* (Nashville, TN: Nelson Books, 2022), ix; and Paulo Coelho, *The Alchemist*, trans. Alan R. Clarke (New York: HarperOne, 1993), 116.

6. Henri Nouwen, *The Way of the Heart: The Spirituality of the Desert Fathers and Mothers* (New York: Ballantine Books, 2003), 18.

7. Martyn Lloyd-Jones, *Seeking the Face of God: Nine Reflections on the Psalms* (Wheaton, IL: Crossway Books, 2005), 34.

8. Peter Scazzero, *The Emotionally Healthy Leader: How Transforming Your Inner Life Will Deeply Transform Your Church, Team, and the World* (Grand Rapids, MI: Zondervan, 2015), 55.

9. Brennan Manning, *Abba's Child: The Cry of the Heart for Intimate Belonging* (Colorado Springs: NavPress, 2015), 17.

10. Dane Ortlund, *Deeper: Real Change for Real Sinners* (Wheaton, IL: Crossway, 2021), 40–41.

11. John Piper, "Our Weakness Reveals His Worth," Bible Gateway Devotional, accessed January 9, 2024, www.biblegateway.com /devotionals/john-piper-devotional/2050/08/02.

12. Ortlund, *Deeper*, 42.

Chapter 3: Coming Home

1. Richard Halloran, "Soldier's Return from Thirty Years in Jungle Stirs Japanese Deeply," *New York Times*, March 13, 1974, www.nytimes.com/1974/03/13/archives/soldiers-return-from -30-years-in-jungle-stirs-japanese-deeply.html.

2. Tim Keller, *The Prodigal God: Recovering the Heart of the Christian Faith* (New York: Riverhead Books, 2011), 36.

3. Keller, *Prodigal God*, 36.

4. Leon Morris, *1 and 2 Thessalonians: An Introduction and Commentary*, vol. 13, Tyndale New Testament Commentaries, 2nd ed. (Downers Grove, IL: InterVarsity Press, 1985), 76–77.

5. Alexander Maclaren, "The Heart's Home and Guide," *Maclaren's Expositions*, Bible Hub, accessed August 19, 2023, https://biblehub .com/commentaries/2_thessalonians/3-5.htm.

6. G. K. Beale and D. A. Carson, eds., *Commentary on the New Testament Use of the Old Testament* (Grand Rapids, MI: Baker Academic, 2007), 308.

7. A. W. Tozer, *The Knowledge of the Holy: The Attributes of God: Their Meaning in the Christian Life* (New York: HarperCollins, 2022), 31.

8. Dane Ortlund, *Deeper: Real Change for Real Sinners* (Wheaton, IL: Crossway, 2021), 86–90.

9. Brennan Manning, *Abba's Child: The Cry of the Heart for Intimate Belonging* (Colorado Springs: NavPress, 2015), 42.

10. Ortlund, *Deeper*, 171.

11. *C. H. Spurgeon's Autobiography*, vol. 1 (London: Passmore and Alabaster, 1897), 105–6.

12. *Spurgeon's Autobiography*, 106.

13. Eugene Peterson, *Practice Resurrection: A Conversation on Growing Up in Christ* (Grand Rapids, MI: Eerdmans, 2010), 1.

Chapter 4: Take Him at His Word

1. Voltaire, quoted in *Oxford Essential Quotations*, ed. Susan Ratcliffe (Oxford: Oxford University Press, 2017), www.oxfordreference .com/display/10.1093/acref/9780191843730.001.0001/q-oro-ed5 -00011218;jsessionid=B2FA9529D0A6B54654AB896C0C0F73FE.

2. William Shakespeare, *Troilus and Cressida* (Yale: Yale University Press, 1927), 38.

3. Tim Keller, *The Reason for God: Belief in an Age of Skepticism* (New York: Penguin Books, 2018), xvi.

4. Tim Keller, "Abraham and the Torch," Gospel in Life, sermon, November 3, 1996, www.youtube.com/watch?v=4MLqalGN_ZQ.

5. John Piper, "The Most Important Promise in My Life," Desiring God, October 23, 2018, www.desiringgod.org/articles/the-most -important-promise-in-my-life.

6. Robert H. Mounce, *Romans*, vol. 27, The New American Commentary (Nashville, TN: Broadman & Holman, 1995), 190.

7. *Speeches by C. H. Spurgeon at Home and Abroad*, ed. Godfrey Holden Pike (London: Passmore & Alabaster, 1878), 17.

Chapter 5: Our Provider

1. Nassim Nicholas Taleb, *Antifragile: Things That Gain from Disorder* (New York: Random House, 2014), 4.

2. Taleb, *Antifragile*, 3.

3. Taleb, *Antifragile*, 43.

Chapter 6: The New Safety

1. Steven M. Southwick and Dennis S. Charney, *Resilience: The Science of Mastering Life's Greatest Challenges* (Cambridge, UK: Cambridge University Press, 2018), 65.

2. Southwick and Charney, *Resilience*, 65.

3. *Letters of John Keats to His Family and Friends*, ed. Sidney Colvin (London: Macmillan, 1891), 54.

4. Tim Keller and Kathy Keller, *The Meaning of Marriage: Facing the Complexities of Commitment with the Wisdom of God* (New York: Penguin Books, 2011), 68.

5. Ben Cost, "Boy Survives Deadly Landslide by Taking Refuge in Fridge," *New York Post*, April 20, 2022, https://nypost.com/2022 /04/20/filipino-boy-survives-deadly-landslide-by-hiding-in-fridge/.

6. "Shelter at Home in the Second World War," History Press, February 24, 2017, www.thehistorypress.co.uk/articles /shelter-at-home-in-the-second-world-war/.

7. Augustine, *The City of God*, trans. Marcus Dods (Edinburgh, UK: T & T Clark, 1871), 98–99.

8. Derek Kidner, *Genesis: An Introduction and Commentary*, vol. 1, Tyndale Old Testament Commentaries (Downers Grove, IL: InterVarsity Press, 2008), 95.

9. Ethelbert W. Bullinger, *The Companion Bible: Being the Authorized Version of 1611 with the Structures and Notes, Critical, Explanatory and Suggestive and with 198 Appendixes*, vol. 1 (Bellingham, WA: Faithlife, 2018), 11.

10. Blue Letter Bible, s.v. "kapar," accessed November 1, 2023, www.blueletterbible.org/lexicon/h3722/kjv/wlc/0-1/.

11. J. I. Packer, *Knowing God* (Downers Grove, IL: InterVarsity Press, 2018), 275.

12. John Piper, "Clyde Kilby's Resolutions for Mental Health and for Staying Alive to God in Nature," Desiring God, August 27, 1990, www.desiringgod.org/articles/clyde-kilbys-resolutions-for-mental-health-and-for-staying-alive-to-god-in-nature.

13. A. W. Tozer, *The Knowledge of the Holy: The Attributes of God: Their Meaning in the Christian Life* (New York: HarperCollins, 2022), 40.

Chapter 7: Walking through Fire

1. Max Roser, "Mortality in the Past: Every Second Child Died," Our World in Data, April 11, 2023, https://ourworldindata.org/child-mortality-in-the-past.

2. Carl R. Trueman, *The Rise and Triumph of the Modern Self: Cultural Amnesia, Expressive Individualism, and the Road to Sexual Revolution* (Wheaton, IL: Crossway, 2020), 50.

3. Peter Scazzero, *Emotionally Healthy Spirituality: It's Impossible to Be Spiritually Mature While Remaining Emotionally Immature* (Grand Rapids, MI: Zondervan, 2017), 117.

4. Scazzero, *Emotionally Healthy Spirituality*, 118.

5. Tim Keller, *The Reason for God: Belief in an Age of Skepticism* (New York: Penguin Books, 2018), 23.

6. G. K. Chesterton, "The Book of Job," in *On Lying in Bed and Other Essays*, ed. Alberto Manguel (Calgary, Canada: Bayeux Arts, 2000), 176.

7. Tim Keller, *Hope in Times of Fear: The Resurrection and the Meaning of Easter* (New York: Viking, 2021), 71.

8. Keller, *Hope in Times of Fear*, 80.

9. Keller, *Hope in Times of Fear*, 187.

10. Scazzero, *Emotionally Healthy Spirituality*, 117.

11. Scazzero, *Emotionally Healthy Spirituality*, 125–36.

12. Scazzero, *Emotionally Healthy Spirituality*, 123.

13. Eugene Peterson, *Practice Resurrection: A Conversation on Growing Up in Christ* (Grand Rapids, MI: Eerdmans, 2010), 8.

Chapter 8: Union with Christ

1. "Amelia Earhart," Britannica, last updated January 2, 2024, www.britannica.com/biography/Amelia-Earhart.

2. Dane Ortlund, *Deeper: Real Change for Real Sinners* (Wheaton, IL: Crossway, 2021), 53–54.

3. Ortlund, *Deeper*, 53.

4. Ortlund, *Deeper*, 54.

5. C. S. Lewis, *Mere Christianity* (New York: Macmillan, 1958), 39.

6. "Union with Christ," Ligonier, March 20, 2022, www.ligonier.org /guides/union-with-christ.

7. Ortlund, *Deeper*, 62.

8. Ortlund, *Deeper*, 57–62.

9. "One God, One People," Ligonier, February 16, 2009, www.ligonier.org/learn/devotionals/one-god-one-people.

10. Ortlund, *Deeper*, 59.

11. Charles Spurgeon, "Solemn Pleadings for Revival," sermon, January 3, 1875, Spurgeon Center for Biblical Preaching at

Midwestern Seminary, www.spurgeon.org/resource-library/sermons
/solemn-pleadings-for-revival-3/#flipbook/.

12. Craig S. Keener, *The IVP Bible Background Commentary: New
Testament*, 2nd ed. (Downers Grove, IL: InterVarsity Press, 2014),
472.

13. Roy E. Ciampa and Brian S. Rosner, *The First Letter to the
Corinthians*, The Pillar New Testament Commentary (Grand Rapids,
MI: William B. Eerdmans, 2010), 261.

14. Henry Scougal, *The Life of God in the Soul of Man* (Fearn,
Scotland: Christian Focus, 1996), 41–42.

15. *The Letters of William James*, ed. Henry James, vol. 2 (Boston:
Atlantic Monthly Press, 1920), 253–54.

Chapter 9: When He Seems Far

1. Saint Augustine, *Confessions* (Oxford, UK: Oxford University
Press, 2008), 1.

2. David Mathis, "We Will See His Face," Desiring God, March 11,
2021, www.desiringgod.org/articles/we-will-see-his-face.

3. Burton Scott Easton, "Presence," ed. James Orr et al., *The
International Standard Bible Encyclopaedia* (Chicago: Howard-
Severance, 1915), 2438.

4. Blue Letter Bible, s.v. "panim," accessed November 1, 2023, www.blueletterbible.org/lexicon/h6440/kjv/wlc/0-1/.

5. Peter Scazzero, *The Emotionally Healthy Leader: How Transforming Your Inner Life Will Deeply Transform Your Church, Team, and the World* (Grand Rapids, MI: Zondervan, 2015), 133.

6. Ruth Haley Barton, *Strengthening the Soul of Your Leadership: Seeking God in the Crucible of Ministry*, 2nd ed. (Downers Grove, IL: InterVarsity Press, 2018), 47.

7. Henri Nouwen, *The Way of the Heart: The Spirituality of the Desert Fathers and Mothers* (New York: Ballantine Books, 2003), 16, emphasis mine.

8. C. S. Lewis, "The Question of God," PBS, accessed January 14, 2023, www.pbs.org/wgbh/questionofgod/transcript/grief .html#:~:text=When%20I%20lay%20these%20questions,to%20 call%20the%20dead%20back.

9. Nouwen, *Way of the Heart*, 53.

10. Nouwen, *Way of the Heart*, 42.

11. John Piper, *When I Don't Desire God: How to Fight for Joy* (Wheaton, IL: Crossway Books, 2004), 178.

12. Donald J. Wiseman, *1 and 2 Kings: An Introduction and Commentary*, vol. 9, Tyndale Old Testament Commentaries (Downers Grove, IL: InterVarsity Press, 1993), 185.

13. A. W. Tozer, *The Pursuit of God* (Grand Rapids, MI: Baker, 2013), 44.

14. Tim Keller, *Hope in Times of Fear: The Resurrection and the Meaning of Easter* (New York: Viking, 2021), 58.

Chapter 10: The Fullness of God

1. G. K. Beale and D. A. Carson, eds., *Commentary on the New Testament Use of the Old Testament* (Grand Rapids, MI: Baker Academic, 2007), 438.

2. *The ESV Study Bible* (Wheaton IL: Crossway, 2008), 1372.

3. Nicholas Carr, *The Shallows: What the Internet Is Doing to Our Brains* (New York: W & W Norton, 2020), 87.

4. Carr, *Shallows*, 6–7.

5. John Eldredge, *Resilient: Restoring Your Weary Soul in These Turbulent Times* (Nashville, TN: Nelson Books, 2022), 138–39.

6. Beale and Carson, *Commentary on the New Testament Use of the Old Testament*, 438.

7. Beale and Carson, *Commentary on the New Testament Use of the Old Testament*, 438.

8. Beale and Carson, *Commentary on the New Testament Use of the Old Testament*, 452.

9. Martyn Lloyd-Jones, *God's Ultimate Purpose: An Exposition of Ephesians 1* (Grand Rapids, MI: Baker, 1978), 349.

10. Beale and Carson, *Commentary on the New Testament Use of the Old Testament*, 454.

11. Dane Ortlund, *Gentle and Lowly: The Heart of Christ for Sinners and Sufferers* (Wheaton, IL: Crossway, 2020), 17.

BURY YOUR ORDINARY

PRACTICAL HABITS OF A HEART FULLY ALIVE

JUSTIN KENDRICK

DAVID **C** COOK™

transforming lives together

INTRODUCTION

I was seventeen years old, sitting on a double-decker bus in Chicago, when God spoke the words that would change my life. It was the second day of a college weekend at a well-known Christian university, and I was hoping to finalize my plans for what I would do after high school. This college had everything I was looking for: courses that interested me, a student body I connected with, and a city that was buzzing with opportunity. I was sitting with a couple of friends I had made over the weekend, each sharing how committed they were to attending the school. Then they turned to me.

"What about you, Justin? Are you going to come here next year?"

That was when God interrupted. I didn't hear an audible voice. I didn't see a flash of lightning. But I did hear something deep inside, almost an inner voice, nudging me in a different direction: *Go home and learn to make disciples.*

What? Go home and do *what*? It seemed crazy. I wasn't even sure what that meant. Yet something inside of me knew what God was calling me to do. I looked up at the Chicago sky and took a deep breath.

"Actually, I don't think so," I said. "I think I need to go home ... to ... *make* disciples ..."

Within a few months, I had enrolled at a state university near my house and had begun a ministry apprenticeship at my local church. People would ask me what my major was at school, and technically I was getting a degree in social work, but I'd sometimes tactlessly answer with an addendum and say, "Truthfully, I'm going to college because I'm trying to figure out how to make disciples." Most people had no idea how to respond. The conversation would usually trail off or abruptly move in a different direction.

I led a few other students to faith in Jesus my first semester, then moved into a dorm on campus and shared a room with three of my new friends. By my senior year, I was living with nine guys in a two-bedroom apartment, all young in faith and learning together to follow Jesus. This was discipleship by trial and error, with a little more error than anything else.

Discipleship is one of those words that Christians use, but it often seems we don't know exactly what it is or how to do it. We know that to be a disciple means to follow Christ, but if we're honest, we aren't completely sure what a disciple actually does or how disciple-making happens. If you ask a mature Christian at your church to "disciple you," he or she will usually meet you for coffee, listen to your problems, and encourage you to read the Bible. Those are all really good things. But is that all there is to discipleship?

How do we live as disciples of Jesus? And how do we leverage our lives to disciple others? Beneath the surface of those questions is another even larger question: How does spiritual growth really work?

This book is the outworking of what I've discovered in the twenty years since that night in Chicago. It is imperfect and incomplete. But it's been tested in the laboratory of real life—first in my own, then in a small group of friends, and finally with thousands of people in a local church context. The results have been nothing short of miraculous. I've had a front-row seat to watch as Christians have seen significant spiritual growth in a short time. Many have finally broken free from destructive patterns, discovered a clearer sense of God's will, and experienced the joy of answered prayer.

Discipleship doesn't need to be a mystery. We can actually create a road map to get us to the destination of spiritual maturity.

When God commanded Adam and Eve to subdue the earth, he gave them authority over creation, but he left a lot of the details for them to discover themselves (Genesis 1:28). He gave no instruction on how to plant corn or herd sheep. He didn't tell them that cotton would be good for making clothes or that cow's milk would be good for drinking. God gave the raw materials to the human race, expecting us to identify and develop systems and routines that produce positive results. It's true that Adam and Eve couldn't make the corn grow, but they could plant the seeds that would lead to a harvest.

In the same way, when Jesus commanded his followers to go and make disciples, he seemed to intentionally leave out some specifics (Matthew 28:19). How exactly do we make a disciple? What do we focus on first? It's true that ultimately all spiritual growth comes from God, but Jesus has given us the raw materials for growth, and he expects us to create the systems and routines that maximize our potential.

This book is a collection of seven spiritual habits. A habit is an acquired pattern of behavior that, when followed regularly, becomes almost involuntary. You've probably had the experience of jumping into your car to run an errand, only to realize that you've somehow taken the route to get to your office instead of the store. It happened without you even thinking about it. This is the power of a habit. If the seven practices described in this book become *habitual*, the spiritual growth that results from them can be exponential.

The first chapter is dedicated to trying to understand the struggle so many Christians are having with spiritual growth. We want to move ahead in our faith but often feel stuck. Next, we'll dissect how growth actually happens according to Scripture. On that foundation, we will build seven spiritual habits, each one building upon the last. (And for more resources, including group study material, check out BuryYourOrdinary.com.)

Before we jump in, let me give you a word of caution from my own life: these habits make me uncomfortable. They challenge my routines, stretch my comfort zones, and nudge me beyond what seems *ordinary* in the Christian life. But if there's one thing we know for certain, it's that the God of the Bible constantly pushes people beyond the ordinary.

This book isn't about adding a few spiritual routines into your already busy life. Rather, it's a field manual to an entirely different way of life in which you dig a deep hole, put the *ordinary you* inside it, cover it with dirt, and walk away. To practice these habits fully, you must bury your ordinary.

Let this serve as an invitation: if you have grown tired of dull spiritual routines and recognize in your heart a hunger for something more, this book is for you. My prayer is that God would use it as fuel on a fire.

Habit: [**hab**-it] *noun:* an acquired
behavior pattern regularly followed until
it has become almost involuntary.

Chapter One

THE ACHE TO BE GREAT

Greatness redefined as relationship with God

"Do you not know that in a race all the runners run, but only one gets the prize? Run in such a way as to get the prize."

1 Corinthians 9:24 NIV

Stan is forty-eight years old and has bounced around between a few churches over the past ten years. He plays bass guitar on the worship team and volunteers with the students for winter camp. He loves God, prays every day, and usually puts money in the basket on Sundays. He doesn't have any really close friends, and he's never told his wife about his occasional struggle with porn. He hesitates to let anyone in on a deeper level. Stan is a good guy, and he wants to grow spiritually. It's just that his brand of spirituality is ... well ... *safe*.

Andre is thirty-two and single. He tries to spend time regularly reading the Bible but often finds himself getting distracted or sucked into the world of social media. Andre lives in the city and stays busy with a thousand hobbies. He dates on and off and always seems to be on the go. He goes to church but recently has found himself inventing excuses to sleep in on Sunday. His spiritual life is lingering in the background of his schedule, but it seems to lack any real initiative. He believes in Jesus, but the fire in his eyes is pretty dim. He does the things that Christians do, but underneath the routine, Andre is ... well ... *bored*.

Monica is twenty-eight and the mother of two little kids. She runs from preschool to gymnastics and rarely has a moment when someone isn't crying or pooping. She fell in love with Jesus when she was in college and even dreamed of moving to the mission field one day, but then she met her husband and adjusted the plan. Those days of big dreams and excitement on a global scale feel like a lifetime ago. Monica talks to God in the margins of her chaotic days, and her faith feels ... well ... *ordinary*.

Have you ever imagined yourself being a part of something really significant? Have you ever written down a dream or a prayer that feels a thousand miles out of reach? There's something inside all of us that desires *more*. We can't completely escape the feeling, but it seems that life often distracts us from directly pursuing the dream. Things pile up and plans change.

These days, maybe you sell homeowner's insurance. Of course, there's nothing wrong with that. It could be a great job that provides for your family. But maybe it's not the dream that's been whispering to your heart for years. Now all you find yourself doing is going through the motions: you finish that college course or you get married and start having kids or you climb the corporate ladder. You love your friends and your family. You even love your church. But it feels as though something important is missing from the equation.

Is it possible that a little honest reflection would confirm that your spiritual life is safe, a little boring, and ... well ... ordinary? Though that quiet whisper is always in the background, you can't seem to get rid of it.

There's got to be more than this.

I recently came across the obituary of Victor Dorman. I never met him personally, but the final words written about him caught my attention.

> Victor Dorman, who helped change the way Americans buy cheese by putting "the paper between the slices" as chairman of the Dorman Cheese Company, died on March 4 at his home in Delray Beach, Fla. He was 80.[4]

To be honest, I appreciate the paper between the slices of cheese as much as anyone. Mr. Dorman appeared to be a successful businessman and may have been a wonderful person. But when I look back at my life and think about someone writing the two final sentences about my existence on Earth, do I want something like this mentioned?

Are you content with the life you're living? Are you content with your current experience of God, or is something on the inside calling you further? Too often, our reaction to this sense of discontentment is to try to satisfy spiritual desires with natural solutions. We tell ourselves that if we just got the right job or met that special someone or had a baby, then life would feel significant. But regardless of how wonderful these things may be, they cannot satisfy the deeper call of the soul.

. . . .

Regardless of how wonderful these things may be, they cannot satisfy the deeper call of the soul.

. . . .

The early church father Augustine got it right when he prayed, "You have made us for yourself, O Lord. And our hearts are restless until they find their rest in you."[5] Have you felt the stirring of a restless heart? It may be hiding under a thick layer of Netflix, new gadgets, and a recent failed attempt at romance—but it's still there under the surface.

How do we actually experience a life full of adventure, purpose, and power? Is that even possible ... or is this all there is?

Remembering Mr. Magic

On my fifth birthday, my parents threw me a party and invited Mr. Magic to our house. In real life, he was a retired art teacher from the neighboring town, but in my mind, Mr. Magic was a sign and a wonder. He had a black top hat, a white cane, and a box full of mysterious things.

At one point in his performance, he dragged me onto his stage (also known as the corner of my living room) and in front of all my friends asked me to stuff his magical handkerchief in the front of my pants. I was wearing my karate suit and quickly obeyed his instructions. He waved his wand, then pulled the handkerchief out. It now had a large pair of white underwear attached to it. The crowd let out an audible "Ahhhhh."

I was stunned. I immediately checked to see if my underwear was still on, and it was! My mind began racing with possible explanations for what had just happened. The underwear now attached to the handkerchief was far larger than anything I had ever worn. I tried to put the pieces together.

Somehow, Mr. Magic had replicated my underwear, increased the size of the new pair, and removed it from my body—all in an instant! Amazing. But how did he do it?

At that moment, I was open to any explanation. My five-year-old mind was like a blank sheet of paper. Maybe his wand had underwear-multiplying capabilities. Maybe the handkerchief was made of some super-special material. Maybe my karate suit had magical powers. At that time in my life, at that moment, the concept of *possibility* was completely pliable.

Life would later teach me that magic wands don't exist, that there are no super-special materials, and that my karate suit was just a $19.99 purchase from Walmart. The magic of what's possible got snuffed out by what's reasonable, and Mr. Magic turned back into a retired art teacher from the neighboring town.

Do you remember your days of imagination? In your wildest, most cherished childhood dreams, what did your future look like? Were you an astronaut? A professional athlete? A movie star? I remember dreaming about being a sailor who would sail a ship around the whole world. I'm sure you had a dream too. But as we got older, we all learned to anchor our dreams in reality. We looked around us and began to expect only what we'd seen others achieve.

This is where the life of Jesus abruptly interrupts our settle-for-less, realistically sized dreams. The accounts of his life describe a man who was constantly stretching the bounds of what was possible. He walked on water, raised the dead, talked to a storm, and cast out demons. In the gospel of Mark, Jesus was confronted by a man whose son was plagued with seizures. The father was desperate for help and cried out to Jesus, "If you can do anything, have compassion on us and help us" (Mark 9:22).

The response of Jesus was startling. "'If you can'! All things are possible for one who believes" (Mark 9:23).

What are we supposed to do with a sentence like that? *All things* are possible? Come on, Jesus; let's be realistic! But he didn't stop there.

"Truly, I say to you, whoever says to this mountain, 'Be taken up and thrown into the sea,' and does not doubt in his heart, but believes that what he says will come to pass, it will be done for him" (Mark 11:23).

In another instance, he said, "Very truly I tell you, whoever believes in me will do the works I have been doing, and they will do even greater things than these, because I am going to the Father" (John 14:12 NIV).

The more I study the life of Jesus, the more convinced I am that he wasn't kidding. He was declaring war on our rational, limited view of reality and demanding that we redraw the lines of what is possible. He doesn't want us to believe that only *he* can do impossible things. He wants us to live as though *we* can do them too.

Jesus invites every believer into something more. More than routines, more than deadlines, more than ordinary. Inside every human being, God has put an *ache to be great*, and the Spirit of Jesus calls each of us to respond.

True Greatness

What does it really mean to be great? The world around us is quick to paint a vivid picture. Our culture teaches us that if you acquire a large pile of money or become famous and well known in society, if you have millions of followers on social media—then you are great. We are told that if you accomplish a noteworthy task or invent something new, if you excel as an athlete, if you get your name in the newspaper, or if you win a special award—then you are great. All of these ideas are shadows of the truth, and they don't capture the real essence of greatness.

If this life is all there is, then we could define greatness by these measurements, but the central message of Jesus is that *this life is not all there is!* You are an eternal being, with an eternal purpose. Beyond what you can see with your natural eyes, there is a spiritual world, and it is the unseen things that last forever. Because of this, true greatness cannot be defined by status or accomplishments in this life. It must be defined by your impact in the next life.

True greatness does not begin with accomplishments. It begins with *relationship.* Jesus shared the secret of greatness when he said, "Now this is eternal life: that they *know you*, the only true God, and Jesus Christ, whom you have sent" (John 17:3 NIV).

Consider the implications of his message. Eternal life is a lot longer than the seventy or eighty years we get on this earth. Jesus just lit on fire our cultural idols of accomplishment and status. According to him, true greatness is relationship with God.

When you zoom out from the chaos of everyday life, this perspective makes perfect sense. In a thousand years, will anyone remember your invention, your hit song, or your successful business? What about in ten thousand years? If God is God and eternity is real, then a great life is one that is lived in authentic, growing relationship with him. To know God, I mean really know him—this is life itself!

But is a vibrant, personal relationship with God a real possibility? To know God ... think about that! Not just to know about him or to know godly principles, but to actually operate daily from a living relationship with him. To hear his voice, to know his heart, and to exist in the center of his plan. This is the bull's-eye of what it means to live a truly great life!

The central message of the gospel is that relationship with God is available to us through the cross of Jesus Christ. He died for your sins, overcame death, and eternally removed the barrier between you and God.

By faith in him, you can know God and live in the center of his will. This is what your heart has been looking for all along in the thirst for status and attention. Those things are imposters, preventing you from realizing what your heart really aches for—relationship with God. Nothing else will satisfy. And through his death and resurrection, Jesus makes that relationship a real possibility.

. . . .

Those things are imposters, preventing you from realizing what your heart really aches for—relationship with God. Nothing else will satisfy.

. . . .

So if the door is actually open, how do we run through it? How do we draw close to God and live a life in which the promises of Jesus become an experiential reality?

In his classic book *Good to Great*, Jim Collins tells the story of Dave Scott, winner of six Ironman Triathlons, and his habit of rinsing his cottage cheese before eating it.[6] Scott believed that the extra rinse would get excess fat off the cheese, sculpting his diet to the most minuscule detail. He wanted to win and reach his full potential so badly that no sacrifice was too great and no detail was too small.

Top-level athletes do things like this all the time, taking their training further and pushing themselves beyond where they've gone before. We hear about this type of dedication, and it doesn't surprise us. If you want to win six Ironman Triathlons, we understand that it's going to require that you embrace some uncommon habits. No one thinks Dave Scott is crazy for his behavior, because he is doing what it takes to win.

If God can really be known, and if a truly great life *is* relationship with him, then why doesn't our pursuit of him reflect this cottage-cheese-rinsing intensity? Why do uncommon habits often seem extreme and unrealistic for the follower of Jesus? When the apostle Paul taught the church in Corinth about living in real relationship with God, he used the analogy of an athlete.

> Do you not know that in a race all the runners run, but only one receives the prize? So run that you may obtain it. Every athlete exercises self-control in all things. They do it to receive a perishable wreath, *but we an imperishable*. (1 Corinthians 9:24–25)

How foolish does a perishable wreath look in comparison to knowing the Creator of the universe? And yet, Dave Scott—who is pursuing an earthly prize—is rinsing his cottage cheese, while many followers of Jesus—who are pursuing an imperishable prize—hesitate to embrace habits that disrupt any of our comforts. If Olympians can show this level of intensity, and all they obtain is a trophy or medal, then what about those who have been promised eternal life? What about those who have access to a real relationship with God and whose actions today have implications forever?

Maybe the missing element to a truly great life has less to do with God's willingness to move and more to do with our unwillingness to move. The greater life we yearn for is actually obtainable, but it's going to take a significant shift in our perspective and behavior to obtain it.

I remember the first time the weight of Jeremiah 29:13 settled on my soul. It's here that God plainly states what it will take to experience real relationship with him in this life: "You will seek Me and find Me when you search for Me with all your heart" (NASB). All your heart. That's what it takes. Half your heart doesn't get you there with God.

Imagine for a minute what your life would look like if this truth were applied, if you actually redirected your attention toward relationship with God as your *central goal in life*. How would life be different if your personal pursuit of him eclipsed your career ambitions, your desire for new comforts, your hobbies, your recreation—even your family and friends?

Does that sound extreme? Of course it does. But in light of the cross and the truth of eternity, it also sounds like the only practical way to live. Something deep on the inside calls out to you right now, even as you read these words, because you were created to do something great. Something *more*. You can't settle for a dull, distant, spiritual life.

The history books of heaven are full of people who took the words of Jesus seriously, and eternity has been shaped through their sacrifice. People like the apostle Paul, Martin Luther, Corrie ten Boom, William Seymour, Jim Elliot, and Dietrich Bonhoeffer. Normal people whose hearts were captured by an eternal purpose. Consider the perspective of Jonathan Edwards, one of history's greatest preachers:

> On the supposition, that there never was to be but one individual in the world, at any one time, who was properly a complete Christian, in all respects of a right stamp, having Christianity always shining in its true luster, and appearing excellent and lovely, from whatever part and under whatever character viewed:

Resolved, To act just as I would do, if I strove with all my might to be that one, who should live in my time.[7]

What an amazing ambition. Edwards was resolved to be the one person in his time who really walked with God. He wasn't waiting for someone else to do it. He took God's invitation seriously and responded with all his heart. But where are the followers of Jesus today who will pick up the baton that Edwards carried?

It's up to you and me. God's Spirit on the inside of us is calling. Will you settle for your current level of spiritual experience, or will you dive deeper? Will you respond to the call of God and even rearrange the way you live so that relationship with him becomes the central goal of your life?

I want to invite you to a funeral. It may sound a little strange, but sometimes a funeral is necessary. At this funeral, we will bury the old ordinary you—your ordinary life, ordinary faith, ordinary prayer, ordinary routines—and replace ordinary with something greater. It will require significant change, but the change is possible by God's Holy Spirit. Everything begins with you saying *yes*.

Jesus, I want a deeper relationship with you. Forgive me for accepting far less than you have made available. Right now, I say yes. Awaken my heart with a passion for you that goes beyond every other passion in my life. I choose to seek you with all my heart.

MORE by JUSTIN KENDRICK

Bury Your Ordinary is a field manual to an entirely different way of life in which you dig a deep hole, put the "ordinary you" inside it, cover it with dirt, and walk away as a new person—the real you.

Through intentional changes to your habits, you will discover a deeper love for God and a deeper understanding of yourself. Be challenged to stretch beyond your comfort zones as you discover:

- Seven habits that lead to explosive spiritual growth
- The one change to your routine that will give you an entirely new way of living
- How our routines can either free us or keep us bound
- The key ingredient God looks for in a disciple-maker
- Why God is already deeply satisfied with who you are

For more, including free small group resources, visit **buryyourordinary.com**

Scan to read the first chapter free!

Available in print, digital, and audio
wherever books are sold

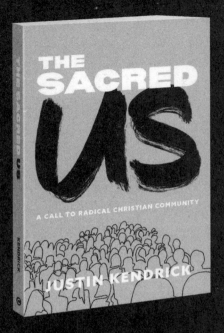